John F. Kennedy
in His Own Words

John F. Kennedy
IN HIS OWN WORDS

EDITED BY

Eric Freedman, J.D., and
Edward Hoffman, Ph.D.

CITADEL PRESS
Kensington Publishing Corp.
WWW.KENSINGTONBOOKS.COM

CITADEL PRESS BOOKS are published by

Kensington Publishing Corp.
850 Third Avenue
New York, NY 10022

All Kensington titles, imprints, and distributed lines are available at special quantity discounts for bulk purchases for sales promotions, premiums, fund-raising, educational, or institutional use. Special book excerpts or customized printings can also be created to fit specific needs. For details, write or phone the office of the Kensington special sales manager: Kensington Publishing Corp., 850 Third Avenue, New York, NY 10022, attn: Special Sales Department; phone 1-800-221-2647.

CITADEL PRESS and the Citadel logo are Reg. U.S. & TM Off.

First printing: October 2005

10   9   8   7   6   5   4   3   2   1

Printed in the United States of America

Library of Congress Control Number: 2005928510

ISBN 0-8065-2632-7

Dedication

★ ★ ★ ★ ★

*In memory of Morris and Charlotte Freedman, members of
John F. Kennedy's Greatest Generation, and for Kiersten
and Aedan, members of a great future generation.* —EF

*To the memory of Roslyn Hoffman and Irwin Hoffman,
members of John F. Kennedy's Greatest Generation, and for
Aaron and Jeremy, members of a great future generation.* —EH

Contents

★ ★ ★ ★ ★

Foreword

by James H. Scheuer

★ ★ ★ ★ ★

With the enthusiasm and inspiration of John F. Kennedy's idealism, I came of political age during his too-brief presidency. I ran unsuccessfully for Congress in 1962, a year before his death, then successfully in 1964, less than twelve months after his assassination. During my quarter century on Capitol Hill, so many of his causes stayed on our agenda, including equal rights, economic growth, educational opportunity, the need for vigilance against terrorism, and the nation's role as a world leader and model for democracy.

Certainly the world has changed with the end of the Cold War, the collapse of the Soviet Union, and the abandonment of the futile war in Southeast Asia. But so many of the same issues confront us now. JFK recognized the need for religious and racial tolerance—and that need is just as pressing today. He recognized the need for decent housing, for health care, for job training, for scientific research, for the arts—and those needs are just as pressing today.

As I reread his words in this insightful collection by Eric Freedman and Edward Hoffman, JFK's ideals demand our continued attention. Those words and ideals should strike at the soul and heart of America and the world, despite the passage of time. His demand—"Ask not what your country can do for you; ask what you can do for your country. My fellow citizens of the world: ask not what America will do for you, but what together we can do for the freedom of man"—remains a clarion call for public service and human rights. His United Nations speech—

"Mankind must put an end to war, or war will put an end to mankind"—is ever timely as we witness violence erupt in region after region, country after country. His warning that "our progress as a nation can be no swifter than our progress in education" is surely true in the 21st century.

James H. Scheuer, a Democrat from New York, was first elected to the U.S. House of Representatives in 1964 and retired at the end of 1992. Like Kennedy, he is a World War II veteran.

Acknowledgments

★ ★ ★ ★ ★

Producing this anthology has been an enjoyable process, but it could not have been accomplished without the valuable help of others. The impetus came from editor Richard Ember of Kensington Publishing; for his vision and encouragement, we are much indebted. Alice Martell, our literary agent, provided the initial enthusiasm for this undertaking. As research assistants, Linda Joyce, Kyung-Mi Song, and Daniel Thai proved consistently efficient.

For many hours of stimulating conversations related to Kennedy's tumultuous life and times, we are grateful to Aaron Hostyk and Dr. Ted Mann.

On our respective home fronts, we owe special gratitude to Mary Ann and to Elaine for providing the support for bringing this project to a successful completion.

★ ★

INTRODUCTION:

Beyond Camelot

★ ★

Beyond the glitter, beyond the nostalgia, beyond the charisma—beyond
Camelot—John F. Kennedy was a remarkable and articulate thinker. As
we look back from a forty-year vantage point at his violently shortened
presidential tenure, we tend to focus on the drama—such as the Cuban
Missile Crisis with its showdown with the Soviet Union—or his bold policy initiatives—such as the Peace Corps—or his assassination and its after-
math.

Unfortunately, such a narrow focus fails to examine the broad range
of Kennedy's ideas and vision, from his college days through his World
War II experiences and in his political career from the House of Representatives to the Senate to the White House. For example, our memory
recalls his bold endorsement of liberty and his trumpet call to the public spirit in his inaugural address on a cold Washington, D.C., morning in
January 1961. That was the speech in which he told his fellow Americans,
"Ask not what your country can do for you—ask what you can do for
your country" and in which he told his fellow citizens of the world, "Ask
not what America will do for you, but what together we can do for the
freedom of man." We also remember the tension of his trip to Berlin at
the height of the Cold War, divided into communist and democratic
zones, where he declared, "All free men, wherever they may live, are citizens of Berlin, and, therefore, as a free man, I take pride in the words
'Ich bin ein Berliner.'"

But Kennedy wrote and said so much more on issues ranging from

1

the plight of the rural poor to the space race, from the hate-spewed violence of racism to the role of religious faith, from the nitty-gritty of governmental reform to the pocketbook issues of recession and unemployment, and from the brass-knuckled realm of partisan politics to the failures of the nation's health system and public schools. As a representative, senator, and president, he wrestled with controversies as divisive as labor strikes, communist-inspired uprisings overseas, welfare and military spending, and events as mundane as White House visits by foreign college students and ceremonial proclamations.

But first, we present a little more about the man himself. John F. Kennedy was born at home in Brookline, Massachusetts, on May 29, 1917, the second son of Irish American, Roman Catholic parents, Rose Fitzgerald Kennedy and Joseph Patrick Kennedy. His mother was well educated and highly religious, attending Mass daily. Her father had served two terms as mayor of Boston and predicted that John's older brother, Joseph Jr., would someday become president. As for John's father, he became a bank president at the age of twenty-five, helped run a shipyard during World War I, and later served as U.S. ambassador to Great Britain and head of the Securities and Exchange Commission. His astute investments made the family wealthy and enabled him to bankroll John's political campaigns. Eventually, there would be nine children, two of whom—Robert and Edward (Ted)—would later follow John to the Senate.

He met, wooed, and, in 1953, wed the socialite Jacqueline Bouvier, who helped add to the White House's Camelot glamour and served as the administration's unofficial minister of culture. They had three children.

Biographer Robert Dallek observed in *An Unfinished Life*, "As with all our most interesting public figures, Kennedy is an elusive character, a man who, like all politicians, worked hard to emphasize his favorable attributes and hide his limitations. He and those closest to him were extraordinarily skillful at creating positive images that continue to shape public impressions."

In revisiting Kennedy's thoughts after so many years, we must consider the times that shaped him. He grew up in a wealthy and politically influential family, survived the Depression, and witnessed the inexorable advance of the fascists in Italy, the Nazis in Germany, and the military rightists in Japan. As a child, as a prep school student, and as a Harvard undergraduate, Kennedy struggled with illnesses that sometimes incapacitated him. He overcame formidable medical obstacles, but he also used outside influence to get into the U.S. Navy after he failed an Army physical, then nearly died on duty in the South Pacific near the Solomon Islands while commanding a PT (patrol torpedo) boat that a Japanese destroyer sank.

The onset of his elective life began in the upheaval of a postwar America with its flood of returning veterans into the workforce and while he still grieved over the combat death of his older brother, Joseph Jr.

World War II had wrought massive changes in the domestic fabric and psyche of the nation. For the first time, large numbers of women were able to secure well-paying jobs—in defense plants and elsewhere—at least until the male veterans returned. Large numbers of black Americans served patriotically and valiantly in the military, yet returned home to segregation and racial hatred in both the North and South.

As a result of the war, the physical and political map of the world had dramatically changed as well. By the time Kennedy took the oath of office in January 1947, representing a Massachusetts congressional district, the power of the British Empire and France had already shrunk. China was wracked by civil war between the communists and the corrupt nationalist rulers. Communist movements were active in Latin America, in Africa, and in Asia, including a place unknown to most Americans, Vietnam. The economies and the infrastructure of Japan and Germany remained devastated. The Korean War loomed not far ahead, with its eventual human toll to the United States alone of more than 33,000 dead, 92,000 wounded, and 15,000 taken prisoner or unaccounted for.

Looking back, we tend to characterize Kennedy as a liberal—and he certainly was more liberal than his Republican rivals and many Southern Democrats, members of his own party. But some social forces were perhaps moving too fast for his comfort. While he supported civil rights, he by no means led the political charge in Congress or even as president. During the 1960 campaign, he was the centrist among Democratic aspirants, definitely to the right of both Senator Hubert Humphrey of Minnesota and former Illinois Governor Adlai Stevenson, the party's 1952 and 1956 nominee. He even turned out to be more conservative on many domestic issues than was Senator Lyndon B. Johnson of Texas, his eventual running mate.

His fascination with foreign affairs reflected both the tenor and events of his times and his personal, longtime interest in distant, exotic places and heroes. He told the visiting president of Pakistan on July 11, 1961, "The Khyber Pass, the fact that Alexander (the Great's) troops moved through your country so many years ago in extending their control into the far reaches of the known earth, the great struggles of the 19th and 20th century on your frontiers—all this had a great effect upon at least one young American growing up." Coupled with his father's ambassadorship and his own travels, his internationalist outlook and backing for the United Nations, the North Atlantic Treaty Organization, the Alliance of Progress in Latin America, and similar multinational efforts come as no surprise.

This book doesn't deal with scandals, real or imagined, nor is it about the serious health problems that Kennedy and his aides hid so well from the American people. However, this book doesn't ignore the reality that an outspoken, earthy, vibrant, even politically vindictive Kennedy existed outside the formality and veneer of speeches, official correspondence, and press conferences. For instance, although he repeatedly praised former French President Charles de Gaulle in public, he revealed his true feelings in a private conversation when he referred to the arrogant military hero and political leader as "that bastard." Such bluntness in private was evident as early as his college days at Harvard University. As a student traveling through Europe in the summer of 1937, he made this undiplomatic but candid diary entry: "The distinguishing mark of the Frenchman is his cabbage breath and the fact that there are no bathtubs.... These French will try and rob you at every turn. France is quite a primitive nation."

And while Kennedy's words often were impassioned, he could turn to understatement as well, as in his observation that Soviet Premier Nikita Khrushchev "does not wish us well, unfortunately." And he could express admiration for those competitors and critics who earned his respect, such as the ultraconservative Arizona senator, Barry Goldwater, who would become the 1964 Republican nominee. "I really like him," Kennedy confided to a friendly journalist, "and if we're licked at least it will be on the issues."

This anthology examines Kennedy's writings for their timeliness and relevance today. Intellectually, he was no slouch. His Harvard senior thesis about British foreign policy was turned into his first book, *Why England Slept*. And while in the Senate, he wrote the best-selling, Pulitzer Prize-winning *Profiles in Courage* about U.S. senators who took political stands that jeopardized their political careers.

This new book selects from a rich trove of material, the literally millions of words Kennedy spoke or wrote. The selections come from sources such as a diary he kept in college; books; letters written in and out of office; speeches on the campaign trail and on the floor of Congress; newspaper and magazine articles he wrote; presidential campaign debates with Vice President Richard Nixon; conversations with friends and aides; formal addresses; proclamations; media interviews; and press conferences. Certainly, others wrote much of what he *said*, particularly by the time he reached the Senate, the presidential campaign circuit, and the White House. But even ghostwritten words *belong* to him because they were intended to reflect his thinking and philosophy.

Thus, we turn to those words to discover or rediscover his vision, to learn lessons, and to understand problems that are as vital now as they were during his lifetime. Can there be any doubt what Kennedy believed when he stood in front of the Capitol at his inauguration and told the world, "Now the trumpet summons us again—not as a call to bear arms, though arms we need—not as a call to battle, though embattled we are—but a call to bear the burden of a long twilight struggle, year in and year out, rejoicing in hope, patient in tribulation—a struggle against the common enemies of man: tyranny, poverty, disease and war itself"?

Note to readers: If a citation doesn't include a city,
John F. Kennedy's remarks were made
in Washington, D.C.

★ ★

CHAPTER I

Looking at History

★ ★

"I know of no way of judging the future but by the past," Patrick Henry declared at the Virginia Convention just before America's Revolutionary War. Throughout John Kennedy's own life, he strongly embraced the same philosophy that history shapes the future. As a young man touring Europe for the first time in the 1930s, he was endlessly fascinated by its historic cities and landscapes. European history not only offered aesthetic delight but also offered considerable insight for statecraft. He wrote his 1940 Harvard thesis on the lessons America should learn from studying Britain's failure to stop Hitler's growing militarization. Later published as the book *Why England Slept*, it was Kennedy's first major intellectual achievement.

During Kennedy's congressional years, he looked actively to history for guidance and inspiration on a wide range of contemporary challenges, ranging from labor-business relations and social welfare to international affairs such as the Cold War and the newly formed United Nations. His speeches and writings made clear his conviction that those who fail to study the past are doomed to repeat it. Reflecting Kennedy's especially keen interest in American history, his 1956 bestseller, *Profiles in Courage*, highlighted the politically bravest senators dating back to our nation's founding through recent times.

7

During Kennedy's presidency, his historical outlook intensified. Thus, he frequently emphasized *the long view* when questioned about unfolding events. More acutely than most of his contemporaries, Kennedy recognized how major foreign policy issues—for example, United States relations with post–World War II Europe, Africa, Southeast Asia, and South America— could be resolved only by accurately understanding history and patiently applying its lessons today.

> A nation reveals itself not only by the men it produces
> but also by the men it honors, the men it remembers.
> —Amherst College, Amherst, Massachusetts,
> October 26, 1963

American Figures

John Quincy Adams (1767–1848) was the sixth U.S. president and the first president to be the son of a president, John Adams (1735–1826).

Though one of the most talented men ever to serve the nation, he had few of the personal characteristics which ordinarily give color and charm to the personality. But there is a fascination and nobility in this picture of a man unbending, narrow and intractable, judging himself more severely than his most bitter enemies judged him, possessing an integrity unsurpassed among the major political figures of our history, and constantly driven onward by his conscience and his deeply felt obligation to be worthy of his parents, their example and their precepts.

His frustrations and defeats in political office—as senator and president—were the inevitable result of this intransigence in ignoring the political facts of life.

Profiles in Courage, 1956

John Quincy Adams was one of the great representatives of that extraordinary breed who have left a memorable impact upon our government and our way of life. Harsh and intractable, like the rocky New England countryside which colored his attitude toward the world at large, the

Puritan [Adams] gave meaning, consistency, and character to the early days of the American Republic. His somber sense of responsibility toward his Creator he carried into every phase of his daily life. He believed that man was made in the image of God, and thus he believed him equal to the extraordinary demands of self-government.

Ibid.

We would admire the courage and determination of John Quincy Adams if he served in the Senate today. We would respect his nonpartisan, nonsectional approach. But I am not so certain that we would like him as a person; and it is apparent that many of his colleagues, on both sides of the aisle, did not. His isolation from either political party, and the antagonisms which he aroused, practically nullified the impact of his own independent and scholarly propositions.

Ibid.

John Adams and his son John Quincy Adams both served as president, but Kennedy was also referring to other illustrious members of their family.

The Adams family was extraordinary not only for the continuity of its achievement but also its diversity. Among them were two presidents, a secretary of the Navy, an industrialist, two authors, a diplomat, yet none is remembered for a single or even one dominant vocation. Among them also were lawyers, conversationalists, authors, scholars, sailors. And each...had a special concern to foster links between government and learning.

Book review in *The American Historical Review*, January 1963

Thomas Hart Benton (1782–1858) was elected four times as senator from Tennessee. His opposition to slavery cost him his senatorial career.

All the Senate knew that Thomas Hart Benton was a rough and tumble fighter off and on the Senate floor—no longer with pistols but with stinging sarcasm, vituperative though learned oratory and bitterly heated debate. He himself was immune to the wounds of those political clashes from which his adversaries retired bleeding and broken.

Profiles in Courage, 1956

The first senator ever to serve thirty consecutive years, Thomas Hart Benton achieved a prominence which no other senator from a new state could claim, and he championed the West with a boundless energy no opposing candidate could match. The Pony Express, the telegraph line and the highways to the interior were among his proud accomplishments—and a transcontinental railroad and fully developed West, rich in population and resources, were among his themes.

Ibid.

No amount of acquired information, bulldog persistence, or ferocious egotism could save Thomas Hart Benton from the tidal wave that engulfed the Senate and his state over one burning issue—slavery. Unfortunately, until it was too late, Benton refused to recognize slavery as a major issue [and] believed that the Missouri Compromise of 1820...had taken it out of politics....He [therefore became] a man without a party, a politician without a recognized platform, and a senator without a constituency.

Ibid.

John C. Calhoun (1782–1850) was a representative and senator from South Carolina, and vice president of the United States.

His speeches, stripped of all excess verbiage, marched across the Senate floor in even columns, measured, disciplined, carrying all before them. Strangely enough, although he had the appearance, especially in his later days, of a fanatic, he was a man of infinite charm and personality. He was reputed to be the best conversationalist in South Carolina, and he won to him through their emotions men who failed to comprehend his closely reasoned arguments. His hold upon the imagination and affection of the entire South steadily grew, and at his death in the midst of the great debate of 1850 he was universally mourned.

Profiles in Courage, 1956

As it must to all legislative bodies, politics came to the United States Senate. As the Federalist party split on foreign policy and Thomas Jefferson resigned from the Cabinet to organize his followers, the Senate became a forum for criticism of the executive branch, and the role of executive council was assumed instead by a Cabinet of men upon whom the president could depend to share his views and be responsible to him.

Ibid.

Henry Clay (1797–1852) was a senator and representative from Kentucky.

Though he lacked the intellectual resources of [Daniel] Webster and [John C.] Calhoun, Henry Clay nevertheless had visions of a greater America beyond those held by either of his famous colleagues. And so, in 1820, 1833 and 1850 he initiated, hammered and charmed through reluctant Congresses the three great compromises that preserved the Union until 1861, by which time the strength of the North was such that secession was doomed to failure.

Profiles in Courage, 1956

Henry Clay, who should have known, said compromise was the cement that held the Union together: "All legislation...is founded upon the principle of mutual concession.... Let him who elevates himself above humanity, above its weaknesses, its infirmities, its wants, its necessities, say, if he pleases, 'I never will compromise'; but let no one who is not above the frailties of our common nature disdain compromise."

Ibid.

Thomas Dooley (1927–1961) was a celebrated American physician who pioneered health care programs in Southeast Asia.

I think all of us have been impressed by the extraordinary example of Dr. Dooley, who went to the farthest reaches of this earth of ours in order to serve people whom we would not ordinarily regard as intimately related to us and so far away. The letter he wrote when he set up his last hospital, and which finally reached its destination, indicated his strong feeling of service. It typified the best of our country.

Remarks on presenting the Dr. Thomas Dooley Medal, June 7, 1962

Sam Houston (1793–1863) was one of Texas's most colorful historical fig-ures. He was commander in chief in its war for independence from Mexico, served as first president of the Republic of Texas, and represented the state as a representative and senator.

Sam Houston was a Democrat of long standing. And Sam Houston was a Southerner by birth, residence, loyalty, and philosophy. But Sam Houston was also Sam Houston, one of the most independent, unique, popular, forceful and dramatic individuals ever to enter the Senate chamber.

The first senator from Texas, his name had long been a household word as commander in chief of those straggling and undermanned Texas volunteers who routed the entire Mexican Army at San Jacinto, captured its general and established the independence of Texas. He had been ac-claimed as the first president of the Independent Republic of Texas, a member of her Congress, and president again before the admission of Texas into the Union as a state.

Profiles in Courage, 1956

The contradictions in the life of Sam Houston a century ago may seem irreconcilable today. Although there are available endless collections of diaries, speeches and letters which throw light on every facet of his life and accomplishments, yet in the center of the stage Houston himself re-mains shadowed and obscured, an enigma to his friends in his own time, a mystery to the careful historian of today.

We may read a letter or a diary in which for a moment he seemed to have dropped his guard, but when we have finished, we know little more than before. No one can say with precision by what star Sam Houston steered—his own, Texas', or the nation's.

Ibid.

Sam Houston combined the moral courage to defend principle and the physical courage to defy danger. He was fiercely ambitious yet at the end he sacrificed for principle all that he had ever won or wanted. He was a Southerner, and yet he steadfastly maintained his loyalty to the Union. He was a slaveholder who defended the right of Northern ministers to petition Congress against slavery. He was a heavy drinker who took the vow of temperance. He was an adopted son of the Cherokee Indians who won his first military honors fighting the Creeks. He was governor of Tennessee but a senator from Texas. He was in turn magnanimous yet vindictive, affectionate yet cruel, eccentric yet self-conscious, faithful yet opportunistic.

But Sam Houston's contradictions actually confirm his one basic, consistent quality: indomitable individualism, sometimes spectacular, sometimes crude, sometimes mysterious but always courageous.

Letter on the launching of the USS *Sam Houston*, February 2, 1961

Thomas Jefferson (1743–1826) was a leading author of the Declaration of Independence and the Constitution before serving as president from 1801–1809.

Benjamin Franklin (1706–1790) was a statesman, inventor, writer, and scientist.

Someone once said that Thomas Jefferson was a gentleman of thirty-two who could calculate an eclipse, survey an estate, tie an artery, plan an edifice, try a cause, break a horse and dance the minuet. Whatever he may have lacked, if he could have his former colleague, Mr. Franklin, here we all would have been impressed.

Remarks Honoring Nobel Winners of the Western Hemisphere, April 29, 1962

George Norris (1861–1944) was a representative and senator from Nebraska.

We should not pretend that he was a faultless paragon of virtue; on the contrary, he was, on more than one occasion, emotional in his deliberations, vituperative in his denunciations, and prone to engage in bitter and exaggerated personal attack instead of concentrating his fire upon the merits of an issue. But nothing could sway him from what he thought was right, from his determination to help all the people, from his hope to save them from the twin tragedies of poverty and war.

Profiles in Courage, 1956

George Norris met with both success and failure in his long tenure in public office, stretching over nearly a half a century of American political life. But the essence of the man and his career was caught in a tribute paid to the Republican senator from Nebraska [Norris] by the Democratic presidential nominee in September 1932:

History asks, "Did the man have integrity!
Did the man have unselfishness?
Did the man have courage?
Did the man have consistency?"

There are few statesmen in America today who so definitely and clearly measure up to an affirmative answer to those four questions as does George W. Norris.

Ibid.

Gifford Pinchot (1865–1946) was governor of Pennsylvania, the first head of the U.S. Forest Service, and the man Kennedy called "the father of American conservation."

He viewed his analysis of the American natural resources scene through the eye of a trained scientist. His career marked the beginning of a professional approach in preserving our national resources. He was a gifted administrator. He was an articulate publicist. He was a tutor of presidents.

In the space of a few short years he made... conservation an accepted virtue, and part of our life which we take for granted today.

Address at the Pinchot Institute for Conservation Studies, Milford, Pennsylvania, September 24, 1963

Franklin Delano Roosevelt (1882–1945) of New York became president in 1933 and died in his fourth term in office.

My earliest recollection, really, of President Roosevelt was a picture I saw after his nomination in 1932 when he came with his sons and sailed along the coast of Maine, and a very magic picture of him sitting at the wheel of a sailboat.

> Remarks at Navy Summer Festival, Brunswick, Maine,
> August 10, 1962

I think all of us were very familiar with the stamp collection. But the fact that he had—in addition to having one of the finest stamp collections in the United States if not in the world, that he also had—in spite of having some other interests in his life, the most unusual collection of naval prints, indicates an extraordinary versatility as well as vitality to which he brought everything that he did.

> Remarks on opening an exhibit of Franklin Delano Roosevelt's
> naval prints, June 27, 1962

Theodore Roosevelt (1858–1919) of New York served as president from 1901–1909.

Theodore Roosevelt and Thomas Jefferson were both men of extraordinary versatility and combined a great many talents. In fact, I would suppose that they covered a wider range than any of the presidents of our history and, with the exception of a few extraordinary Americans such as Benjamin Franklin, more than any other Americans of our history.

And it is interesting that Theodore Roosevelt—whose vitality, whose vigor, were such pronounced qualities and such obvious qualities in his administration—was also, with Thomas Jefferson, the president of the United States most concerned with restoring the White House, with the architecture of the White House, with maintaining the spirit of the White House.

> Remarks at the dedication of the restored mantelpiece in the
> State Dining Room of the White House, July 2, 1962

When Theodore Roosevelt became president after being vice president, the leader of his state said, "My God, they've put that cowboy in the White House." Well, because he had been a cowboy in North Dakota and had spent some of the most significant years of his life there, he became committed to the development of the resources of the West. And every citizen who lives in the West owes Theodore Roosevelt, that cowboy, a debt of obligation.

> Remarks following approval of the Fryingpan-Arkansas
> Water Project, Pueblo, Colorado, August 17, 1962

Edmund G. Ross (1826–1907) of Kansas was a leading opponent of slavery. As senator, he cast the deciding vote against the impeachment of President Andrew Johnson.

Who was Edmund G. Ross? Practically nobody. Not a single public law bears his name, not a single history book includes his picture, not a single list of Senate "greats" mentions his service. His one heroic deed has been all but forgotten. But who might Edmund G. Ross have been? That is the question—for Ross, a man with an excellent command of words, an excellent background for politics and an excellent future in the Senate, might well have outstripped his colleagues in prestige and power throughout a long Senate career. Instead, he chose to throw all of this away for one act of conscience.

> *Profiles in Courage,* 1956

I could not close the story of Edmund Ross without some more adequate mention of those six courageous Republicans who stood with Ross and braved denunciation to acquit President Andrew Johnson. Edmund Ross, more than any of those six colleagues, endured more before and after his vote, reached his conscientious decision with greater difficulty, and aroused the greatest interest and suspense prior to [the impeachment conviction vote] by his noncommittal silence. His story, like his vote, is the key to the impeachment tragedy. But all seven of the Republicans who voted against conviction should be remembered for their courage. Not a single one of them ever won re-election to the Senate. Not a single one of them escaped the unholy combination of threats, bribes, and coercive tactics by which their fellow Republicans attempted to intimidate their votes; and not a single one of them escaped the terrible torture of vicious criticism engendered by their vote to acquit.

Ibid.

Sam Rayburn (1882–1961), a Texas Democrat, was Speaker of the House of Representatives from 1940–1961, including Kennedy's time there.

Presidents of both parties pay equal tribute to him. While his devotion to his own party was never questioned, nevertheless he saw in a larger sense the necessity for harmonious relations between the various branches of the government....

No monument, no memorial, no statue would please him half so much, I believe, as to have his name preserved here in this fashion on Capitol Hill. The Congress was his life, the House was his home, and he not only served it far longer than any who preceded him but with distinction and wisdom as well.

Remarks at the cornerstone-laying ceremony of the Rayburn House Office Building, May 24, 1962

Robert A. Taft (1889–1953) was a representative and senator from Ohio.

This son of a former president... was a man who stuck fast to the basic principles in which he believed—and when those fundamental principles were at issue, not even the lure of the White House, or the possibilities of injuring his candidacy, could deter him from speaking out. He was an able politician, but on more than one occasion he chose to speak out in defense of a position no politician with like ambition would have endorsed.

He was, moreover, a brilliant political analyst, who knew that during his lifetime the number of American voters who agreed with the fundamental tenets of his political philosophy was destined to be a permanent minority, and that only by flattering new blocs of support—while carefully refraining from alienating any group which contained potential Taft voters—could he ever hope to attain his goal. Yet, he frequently flung to the winds the very restraints his own analysis advised, refusing to bow to any group, refusing to keep silent on any issue.

Profiles in Courage, 1956

Daniel Webster (1782–1852) was a representative and senator. Serving for thirty-eight years, he was influential for his nationalism.

There could be no mistaking he was a great man—he looked like one, talked like one, was treated like one and insisted he was one. With all his faults and failings, Daniel Webster was undoubtedly the most talented figure in our congressional history: not in his ability to win men to a cause—he was no match in that with Henry Clay; not in his ability to hammer out a philosophy of government—Calhoun outshone him there; but in his ability to make alive and supreme the latent sense of oneness, of Union, that all Americans felt but which few could express.

Profiles in Courage, 1956

A very slow speaker, hardly averaging a hundred words a minute, Webster combined the musical charm of his deep organ-like voice, a vivid imagination, an ability to crush his opponents with a barrage of facts, a confident and deliberate manner of speaking and a striking appearance to make his orations a magnet that drew crowds hurrying to the Senate chamber. He prepared his speeches with the utmost care, but seldom wrote them out in a prepared text. It has been said that he could think out a speech sentence by sentence, correct the sentences in his mind without the use of a pencil, and then deliver it exactly as he thought it out.

Certainly that striking appearance was half the secret of his power, and convinced all who looked upon his face that he was born to rule.

Ibid.

It was because Daniel Webster conscientiously favored compromise in 1850 that he earned a condemnation unsurpassed in the annals of political history. His is a story worth remembering today.

Ibid.

Woodrow Wilson (1856–1924) was president during and after World War I, serving from 1912–1919. He called for a New Freedom at home and a world of unity and peace, and we are still striving to achieve these objectives.

"Democratic institutions are never done," he once wrote. "They are, like the living tissue, always a-making. It is a strenuous thing, this of living the life of a free people, and we cannot escape the burden of our inheritance."

Statement on the Woodrow Wilson Memorial Commission, October 4, 1961

John Peter Zenger (1697–1746) was a German-born journalist in colonial New York who fought for freedom of the press.

When I was growing up, I used to have the greatest admiration for [John] Peter Zenger, who was the great German editor who criticized the (British) colonial government in pre-revolutionary America. His trial was a very famous event.... It helped cause the Revolution.

Toast to President Heinrich Lübke at Villa Hammerschmidt, Bonn, Germany, June 24, 1963

International Figures

Stanley Baldwin (1867–1947) was prime minister of Great Britain in the mid-
1930s, shortly before Kennedy's father served as U.S. ambassador to the
Court of St. James.

From reading numbers of his speeches and comments on him from
friends and critics alike, I think that there can be no doubt that Baldwin
was a master political tactician.... What I think he was trying to show—
and he used the election [of 1933] as the best barometer of a modern
democratic state's popular will—(was) the impossibility of having gotten
support for any rearmament in the country due to the overwhelmingly
pacifist sentiment of the country during those years.

"Appeasement at Munich," Harvard University Thesis, 1940

Christopher Columbus (1451–1506) was an Italian-born explorer who sailed
on behalf of Spain.

I think Columbus has been a fascinating figure to me for many reasons,
but partly because of his extraordinary skill as a navigator....I would
think Columbus would have to be considered the foremost sailor not of
his time but, I think, in history. But the more significant fact, of course, is
the perseverance....

The second voyage, I suppose, may have been more difficult, speaking
as a sailor, and the third one more difficult even than that, particularly
the exploration of the Central American coast.

But of course the more difficult one was the first voyage. That is always true, the first voyages are the hard ones and they require the perseverance and character.

Remarks at Columbus Day Ceremony, October 12, 1963

Gilbert du Motier (Marquis de Lafayette, 1757–1834) was a French soldier and
statesman who fought for the American colonies in the Revolutionary War.

It seems that almost every Frenchman who comes to the United States feels that Lafayette was a rather confused sort of ineffectual, elderly figure, hovering over French politics, and is astonished to find that we regard him as a golden, young romantic figure, next to George Washington our most distinguished citizen.

> Toast to André Malraux, French Minister for Cultural Affairs, May 11, 1962

Casimir Pulaski (1747–1779) was a Polish freedom fighter who died in Savannah, Georgia, aiding colonial forces against the British.

One hundred and eighty-three years ago this month General Casimir Pulaski died. He was only thirty-two. He was not an American. He had been on these shores for less than two years. He represented a different culture, a different language, a different way of life. But he had the same love of liberty as the people of this country and, therefore, he was an American as much as he was a Pole.

> Remarks at the Pulaski Day Parade, Buffalo, New York, October 14, 1962

Leonardo da Vinci (1452–1519) was a Florentine artist, one of the great masters of the High Renaissance, who was also an innovator in many other fields.

Leonardo da Vinci was not only an artist and a sculptor, an architect and a scientist, and a military engineer, an occupation which he pursued, he tells us, in order to preserve the chief gift of nature, which is liberty.

> Remarks at the opening of the Mona Lisa exhibit, National Gallery of Art, January 8, 1963

Immigration in America

People from Europe came to my country for three reasons: either because of famine and a denial of opportunity, or because of their desire for religious freedom, or because of their desire for political freedom.

Remarks at the Romerberg, Frankfurt, Germany, June 25, 1963

From the start, immigration policy has been a prominent subject of discussion in America. This is as it must be in a democracy, where every issue should be freely considered and debated.

Immigration, or rather the British policy of clamping down on immigration, was one of the factors behind the colonial desire for independence. Restrictive immigration policies constituted one of the charges against King George III expressed in the Declaration of Independence. And in the Constitutional Convention, James Madison noted, "That part of America which has encouraged [the immigrants] has advanced most rapidly in population, agriculture and the arts."

So, too, Washington in his Thanksgiving Day Proclamation of 1795 asked all Americans "humbly and fervently to beseech the kind Author of these blessings…to render this country more and more a safe and propitious asylum for the unfortunate of other countries."

Yet there was the basic ambiguity which older Americans have often showed toward newcomers. In 1797 a member of Congress argued that, while a liberal immigration policy was fine when the country was new and unsettled, now that America had reached its maturity and was fully populated, immigration should stop—an argument which has been repeated at regular intervals throughout American history.

A Nation of Immigrants, 1964

People migrated to the United States for a variety of reasons. But nearly all shared two great hopes: the hope for personal freedom and the hope for economic opportunity. In consequence, the impact of immigration has been broadly to confirm the impulses in American life demanding more political liberty and more economic growth.

So, of the fifty-six signers of the Declaration of Independence, eighteen were of non-English stock and eight were first-generation immigrants. Two immigrants—the West Indian Alexander Hamilton, who was Washington's Secretary of the Treasury, and the Swiss Albert Gallatin, who held the same office under Jefferson—established the financial policies of the young republic.

Ibid.

On May 11, 1831, Alexis de Tocqueville, a young French aristocrat, disembarked in the bustling harbor of New York City. He had crossed the ocean to try to understand the implications for European civilization of the new experiment in democracy on the far side of the Atlantic. In the next nine months, Tocqueville and his friend Gustave de Beaumont traveled the length and breadth of the eastern half of the continent—from Boston to Green Bay and from New Orleans to Quebec—in search of the essence of the American way of life.

Tocqueville was fascinated by what he saw. He marveled at the energy of the people who were building the new nation. He admired many of the new political institutions and ideals. And he was impressed most of all by the spirit of equality that pervaded the life and customs of the people.

Though he had reservations about some of the experiences of this spirit, he could discern its workings in every aspect of American society—in politics, business, personal relations, culture, thought. This commitment to equality was in striking contrast to the class-ridden society of Europe. Yet Tocqueville believed "the democratic revolution" to be irresistible.

Ibid.

Immigration plainly was not always a happy experience. It was hard on the newcomers, and hard as well on the communities to which they came. When poor, ill-educated, and frightened people disembarked in a strange land, they often fell prey to native racketeers, unscrupulous businessmen and cynical politicians. William Marcy Tweed [a political boss in New York City] said, characteristically, in defense of his own depredations in the 1870s, "This population is too hopelessly split into races and factions to govern it under universal suffrage, except by bribery of patronage or corruption."

But the very problems of adjustment and assimilation presented a challenge to the American idea—a challenge which subjected that idea to stern testing and eventually brought out the best qualities in American society.

Ibid.

So, too, in the very way we speak, immigration has altered American life. In greatly enriching the American vocabulary, it has been a major force in establishing "the American language," which, as H. L. Mencken demonstrated thirty years ago, had diverged materially from the mother tongue as spoken in Britain.

Even the American dinner table has felt the impact. One writer has suggested that "typical American menus" might include some of the following dishes: "Irish stew, chop suey, goulash, chile con carne, ravioli, knackwurst mit sauerkraut, Yorkshire pudding, Welsh rarebit, borsch, gefilte fish, Spanish omelet, caviar, mayonnaise, antipasto, baumkuchen, English muffins, Gruyère cheese, Danish pastry, Canadian bacon, hot tamales, wiener schnitzel, petits fours, spumone, bouillabaisse, maté, scones, Turkish coffee, minestrone, filet mignon."

Ibid.

Today, many of our newcomers are from Mexico and Puerto Rico. We sometimes forget that Puerto Ricans are U.S. citizens by birth and therefore cannot be considered immigrants. Nonetheless, they often receive the same discriminatory treatment and opprobrium that were faced by other waves of immigrants. The same things are said today of Puerto Ricans and Mexicans that were once said of Irish, Italians, Germans, and Jews. "They'll never adjust; they can't learn the language; they won't be absorbed."

Ibid.

The wisest Americans have always understood the significance of the immigrant. Among the "long train of abuses and usurpations" that impelled the framers of the Declaration of Independence to the fateful step of separation was the charge that the British monarch had restricted immigration: "He has endeavoured to prevent the population of these States; for that reason obstructing the Laws for the Naturalization of Foreigners; refusing to pass others to encourage their migrations hither, and raising the conditions of new Appropriations of Lands."

Ibid.

Immigration policy should be generous; it should be fair; it should be flexible. With such a policy we can turn to the world, and to our own past, with clean hands and a clear conscience. Such a policy would be but a reaffirmation of old principles.

It would be an expression of our agreement with George Washington that, "the bosom of America is open to receive not only the opulent and respectable stranger, but the oppressed and persecuted of all nations and religions, whom we shall welcome to a participation of all our rights and privileges, if by decency and propriety of conduct they appear to merit the enjoyment."

Ibid.

America is a complicated country with tremendous problems as a society which has made itself into one out of many, particularly in the last sixty-five years when a flood of immigrants came to this country—Italian, Irish, German, Scandinavian, French—and built a society which has very strong roots in Europe but which is in a sense unique.

Remarks Welcoming a Group from Valdagno, Italy, May 17, 1963

[The immigrant drive] has been the foundation of American inventiveness and ingenuity, of the multiplicity of new enterprises, and of the success in achieving the highest standard of living anywhere in the world.

A Nation of Immigrants, 1964

CHAPTER 2

Faith and Religion

"I never will, by any word or act, bow to the shrine of intolerance, or admit a right of inquiry into the religious opinions of others," President Thomas Jefferson vowed in 1803. Such radical sentiments at the time were immensely controversial and created many bitter enemies who caustically charged that he was anti-Christian in outlook and therefore unfit for political leadership.

As John Kennedy noted in his book *Why England Slept*, nations are even slower to change their values than individuals. Hence, it is hardly surprising that his religious background aroused so much antipathy when he campaigned for president more than 130 years after Jefferson's death. To millions of Americans, the notion of anyone but a Protestant occupying the nation's highest office was inconceivable. Many worried that Kennedy would "take orders from the Pope" rather than obey the U.S. Constitution on matters of church and state.

The United States in 1960 finally proved ready to elect a Catholic as president, as it had not been in 1928 when Democrat Alfred E. Smith ran. But Kennedy's words and conduct were a vital force in advancing national religious tolerance. Speaking at sectarian as well as interfaith organizations, he offered an authentic voice for respecting each individual's right to believe, worship, and congregate solely according to personal preference.

With earnestness and conviction—and often employing gentle humor as well—Kennedy accomplished more than any elected official of the post–World War II era did to combat religious prejudice and create a nation hospitable to a diversity of faiths.

Religion in American Life

I believe in an America where the separation of church and state is absolute—where no Catholic prelate would tell the President (should he be Catholic) how to act, and no Protestant minister would tell his parishioners for whom to vote—where no church or church school is granted any public funds or political preference.

> —Address to the Greater Houston Ministerial Association,
> September 12, 1960

The problems we face are complex; the pressures are immense, and both the perils and the opportunities are greater than any nation ever faced. In such a time, the limits of human endeavor become more apparent than ever. We cannot depend solely on our material wealth, on our military might, on our intellectual skill or physical courage to see us safely through the seas that we must sail in the months and years to come.

Along with all of these we need faith. We need the faith with which our first settlers crossed the sea to carve out a state in the wilderness, a mission they said in the Pilgrims' Compact, the Mayflower Compact, undertaken for the glory of God....

We are all builders of the future, and whether we build as public servants or private citizens, whether we build at the national or the local level, whether we build in foreign or domestic affairs, we know the truth of the ancient Psalm, "Except the Lord build the house, they labour in vain that build it."

> Remarks at the 11th Annual Presidential Prayer Breakfast,
> February 7, 1963

I think it is appropriate that we pay tribute to this great constitutional principle which is enshrined in the First Amendment of the Constitution: the principle of religious independence, of religious liberty, of religious freedom. But I think it is also important that we pay tribute and acknowledge another great principle, and that is the principle of religious conviction. Religious freedom has no significance unless it is accompanied by conviction....

No man who enters upon the office to which I have succeeded can fail to recognize how every president of the United States has placed special reliance upon his faith in God. Every president has taken comfort and courage when told, as we are told today, that the Lord "will be with thee. He will not fail thee nor forsake thee. Fear not—neither be thou dismayed."

> Remarks to International Christian Leadership, Inc.,
> February 9, 1961

Let us renew the spirit of the Pilgrims at the first Thanksgiving, lonely in an inscrutable wilderness, facing the dark unknown with a faith borne of their dedication to God and a fortitude drawn from their sense that all men were brothers.

Let us renew that sprit by offering our thanks for the uncovenanted mercies, beyond our desert or merit, and by resolving to meet the responsibilities placed upon us.

Let us renew that spirit by sharing the abundance of this day with those less fortunate, in our own land and abroad. Let us renew that spirit by seeking always to establish larger communities of brotherhood.

> Thanksgiving Day proclamation, November 7, 1962

In the area of religion, all the major American faiths were brought to this country from abroad. The multiplicity of sects established the American tradition of religious pluralism and assured to all the freedom of worship and separation of church and state pledged in the Bill of Rights.

> *A Nation of Immigrants,* 1964

I am fully aware of the fact that the Democratic Party, by nominating someone of my faith, has taken on what many regard as a new and hazardous risk—new, at least since 1928. But I look at it this way: the

Democratic Party has once again placed its confidence in the American people, and in their ability to render a free, fair judgment. And you have, at the same time, placed your confidence in me, and in my ability to render a free, fair judgment—to uphold the Constitution and my oath of office—and to reject any kind of religious pressure or obligation that might directly or indirectly interfere with my conduct of the Presidency in the national interest. My record of fourteen years supporting public education—supporting complete separation of church and state—and resisting pressure from any source on any issue should be clear by now to everyone.

I hope that no American, considering the really critical issues facing this country, will waste his franchise by voting either for me or against me solely on account of my religious affiliation. It is not relevant. I want to stress, what some other political or religious leader may have said on this subject. It is not relevant what abuses may have existed in other countries or in other times. It is not relevant what pressures, if any, might conceivably be brought to bear on me. I am telling you now what you are entitled to know: that my decisions on any public policy will be my own—as an American, a Democrat and a free man.

Democratic nomination acceptance apeech,
Los Angeles, July 15, 1960

Whatever issue may come before me as president, if I should be elected—on birth control, divorce, censorship, gambling or any other subject—I will make my decision in accordance with these views, in accordance with what my conscience tells me to be in the national interest and without regard to outside religious pressure or dictate. And no power or threat of punishment could cause me to decide otherwise.

But if the time should ever come—and I do not concede any conflict to be remotely possible—when my office would require me to either violate my conscience or violate the national interest, then I would resign the office, and I hope any other conscientious public servant would do likewise.

But I do not intend to apologize for these views to my critics of either Catholic or Protestant faith, nor do I intend to disavow either my views or my church in order to win this election.

Address to the Greater Houston Ministerial Association,
September 12, 1960

Federal aid should go only to public schools. The principle of church–State separation precludes aid to parochial schools, and private schools enjoy the abundant resources of private enterprises.

Interview with *New York Herald Tribune*,
published September 25, 1960

I've never felt that we should attempt to use the great impulse towards God and towards religion, which all people feel, as an element in a Cold War struggle. Rather, it's not an arm, it is the essence of the issue—not the organization of economy so much, but as the supremacy of moral law, and therefore the right of the individual, his rights to be protected by the state and not be at the mercy of the state.

Remarks to the trustees of the Union of American Hebrew
Congregations, November 13, 1961

May I add this final thought in this week of Thanksgiving: there is much for which we can be grateful as we look back to where we stood only four weeks ago [with the Cuban missile crisis]: the unity of this hemisphere, the support of our allies, and the calm determination of the American people. These qualities may be tested many more times in this decade, but we have increased reason to be confident that these qualities will continue to serve the cause of freedom with distinction in the years to come.

Press conference, November 20, 1962

For many, the world seems to have little changed in the thousands of years of man's hoping and man's suffering. Tyranny walks abroad, and there is fear on the doorsteps of many houses. Yet this much has changed. Freedom has greater strength than in the past.

And the condition toward which men have aspired for centuries—the dignity of mind and expression, the attainment of economic security without the loss of individual integrity—have been historically demonstrated as realities. It is well for free men everywhere to taste again of the suffering of the past through memory and celebration, for this makes present conviction firmer. A stern heritage is a good teacher.

Confident that nothing of man's travail is lost, that the moment of trial is necessary to the moment of victory, and that our path leads out from the City of Man to that of God, the alliance of free men will persevere. In that spirit and kinship, I offer my best wishes.

> Passover message to the National Committee for Labor Israel, New York, April 2, 1961

[The Supreme Court's decision banning prayer in the schools offers] a very easy remedy and that is to pray ourselves. And I would think that it would be a welcome reminder to every American family that we can pray a good deal more at home, we can attend our churches with a good deal more fidelity, and we can make the true meaning of prayer much more important in the lives of all our children. That power is very much open to us.

> Press conference, June 27, 1962

Promoting Religious Tolerance

This morning I had a meeting at the White House which included some of our representatives from far off countries in Africa and Asia. They were returning to their posts for the Christmas holidays. Talking with them afterwards, I was struck by the fact that in the far off continents Moslems, Hindus, Buddhists, as well as Christians, pause from their labors on the 25th of December to celebrate the birthday of the Prince of Peace. There could be no more striking proof that Christmas is truly the universal holiday of all men. It is the day when all of us dedicate our thoughts to others; when all are reminded that mercy and compassion are the enduring virtues; when all show, by small deeds and large and by acts, that it is more blessed to give than to receive.

> Remarks at the Pageant of Peace ceremonies, December 17, 1962

It has always seemed to me that when we all—regardless of our particular religious convictions—draw our guidance and inspiration, and really in a sense moral direction from the same general area, the Bible, the Old and the New Testaments, we have every reason to believe that our various religious denominations should live together in the closest harmony.

We have a great advantage, really, in so much of the world, in having such common roots, and therefore though our convictions may take us in different directions in our faith, nevertheless the basic presumption of the moral law, the existence of God, man's relation to Him—there is generally consensus on those questions.

So that we should set a happy model for the world, but like all things, these things cannot be taken for granted.

Remarks to the National Conference of Christians and Jews,
November 21, 1961

Brotherhood, tolerance, enlightened relations between members of different ethnic groups—these are, after all, simply an extension of the concept upon which all free organized society is based. Some call this concept comity. Some find it in the Golden Rule, others in Rosseau's "social contract." Our Declaration of Independence calls it "the consent of the governed." The ancient Romans called it "civitas filia," or civic friendship.

It is upon this principle and practice, by whatever name it may be called and regardless of what form it takes, that free societies function, governments operate, and orderly, amicable relations between civilized human beings go on. For although the continued presence of sanctions is a necessary part of any legal structure, we depend, in the last analysis not upon our police force and our jails for the preservation of law and order, but upon voluntary observance and self-restraint.

Addressing the Brotherhood Week observance of the
National Conference of Christians and Jews,
Cleveland, Ohio, February 24, 1957

I do not suggest that religion is an instrument of the Cold War. Rather it is the basis of the issue which separates us from those who make themselves our adversary. And at the heart of the matter, of course, is the position of the individual—his importance, his sanctity, his relationship to his fellow men, his relationship to his country and his state. This is in essence the struggle, and it is necessary, therefore, that in these difficult days, when men and women who have strong religious convictions are beleaguered by those who are neither hot nor cold, or by those who are icy cold, it is most important that we make these common efforts.

Remarks at 10th Annual Presidential Prayer Breakfast,
March 1, 1962

In every celebration of ending and beginning there is both the remembrance of tribulation and the anticipation of good.

There is, too, the knowledge that suffering must make a people and a man more certain of the right, while triumph brings with it the command to respect that right.

We have learned that tolerance and cooperation are the ways to true national strength. Americans of the Jewish faith have given their country a great gift in this regard.

Message to American Jewry on Rosh Hashannah
(Jewish New Year), September 6, 1961

The search for freedom of worship has brought people to America from the days of the Pilgrims to modern times. In our own day, for example, anti-Semitic and anti-Christian persecution in Hitler's Germany and the communist empire have driven people from their homes to seek refuge in America. Not all found what they sought immediately. The Puritans of the Massachusetts Bay Colony, who drove Roger Williams and Anne Hutchinson into the wilderness, showed as little tolerance for dissenting beliefs as the Anglicans of England had shown to them. Minority religious sects, from the Quakers and Shakers through the Catholics and Jews to the Mormons and Jehovah's Witnesses, have at various times suffered both discrimination and hostility in the United States.

But the very diversity of religious belief has made for religious toleration. In demanding freedom for itself, each sect had increasingly to permit freedom for others. The insistence of each successive wave of immigrants upon its right to practice its religion helped make freedom of worship a central part of the American creed. People who gambled their lives on the right to believe in their own God would not lightly surrender that right in a new society.

A Nation of Immigrants, 1964

CHAPTER 3

Public Service

Public service was central to John Kennedy's perspective on life and, certainly, among his most cherished values. More than forty years after his death, it is an outlook that continues to inspire countless individuals who heard his strident call for self-sacrifice as the very highest trait of what it means to be an American and, in larger terms, a free person in the world.

Born into recent American aristocracy, nothing would have been easier than for Kennedy to adopt an idle, rich lifestyle. Surely many of his wealthy peers did so. But such a temptation never seemed to have seriously enticed him once past his adolescence. For despite debilitating health problems, including an ulcer, asthma, and an injured back, Kennedy in mid-1941 succeeded through his father's influence in getting accepted into the U.S. Navy.

What was his goal? Why take such a risk? As biographer Thomas Reeves, a staunch Kennedy critic, would concede decades later, "Patriotism was undoubtedly a motive. Then, too, the ambassador's boys had been trained since infancy to face a challenge with unflinching courage."

Soon after his older brother, Joseph Jr., was tragically killed during World War II, John Kennedy instead became carefully groomed for a political career by their ambitious father. But the evidence suggests that even if Joseph

Jr. had chosen public service to occupy his life, John would have done likewise. Indeed, his younger brothers Robert and Edward (Ted) followed this identical path.

Our thirty-fifth president's emphasis on self-sacrifice—surrendering one's ego and comfort for the greater good—undoubtedly was basic to the worldview of many who comprised what historians call "the Greatest Generation" of American history. Idealistically, participating in Franklin D. Roosevelt's crusading New Deal and then fighting globally for U.S. freedom were unforgettable, shared generational experiences.

But in retrospect what made Kennedy's call for public service in such innovative programs as the Peace Corps so compelling—and even inspiring—was the unique ardor, commitment, and personal conviction with which he articulated his outlook.

And so, my fellow Americans, ask not what your country can do for you; ask what you can do for your country.

Inaugural Address, January 20, 1961

I therefore propose...a Peace Corps of talented young men and women, willing and able to serve their country...for three years as an alternative or as a supplement to peacetime selective service, well qualified through rigorous standards, well trained in the languages, skills, and customs they will need to know....

We cannot discontinue training our young men as soldiers of war, but we also want them to be ambassadors of peace.

Campaign address in San Francisco, November 2, 1960

Life in the Peace Corps will not be easy. There will be no salary and allowances will be at a level sufficient only to maintain health and meet basic needs. Men and women will be expected to work and live alongside the nationals of the country in which they are stationed—doing the same work, eating the same food, talking the same language.

But if the life will not be easy, it will be rich and satisfying.

Statement upon signing the order establishing the Peace Corps, March 1, 1961

How many of you are willing to spend 10 years in Africa or Latin America or Asia working for the United States and working for freedom? How many of you who are going to be doctors are willing to spend your days in Ghana? Technicians or engineers: How many of you are willing to work in the Foreign Service and spend your lives traveling around the world? On your willingness to do that, not merely to serve one or two years in the service, but on your willingness to contribute part of your life to this country I think will depend the answer whether we as a free society can compete. I think we can, and I think Americans are willing to contribute. But the effort must be far greater than we have made in the past.

Speech at the University of Michigan, Ann Arbor, October 14, 1960

So as I said a year ago in assuming the presidency, no generation has ever borne a greater responsibility than this generation, and as a member of it, I welcome that responsibility—because it puts us in the front line of the security of the United States and to assist others who also want to be free.

Remarks to members of the American Legion, March 1, 1962

All of us cannot serve in our armed forces or in the government, but there is one thing each of us can do, and that is to take part in our democracy, to participate in it, and we can do that on Tuesday,...which is Election Day.

Statement urging citizens to vote, November 3, 1962

This is a free society and a free economy, and we do believe that freedom and, really, progress is best served by permitting people to advance their private interests, and the combination of this great effort, we believe, advances the public interest. But I don't think that there's any American who would stop there and feel that the public interest is served alone by serving one's private interest.

I think all of us have a public obligation, all of us owe some of our lives and some of our effort to the advancement of the interests of our society, particularly when our society bears such heavy burdens as it does here and around the world.

Remarks to the Advertising Council, March 7, 1962

The Peace Corps, it seems to me, gives us an opportunity to emphasize a very different part of our American character, and that which has really been the motivation for American foreign policy, or much of it, since Woodrow Wilson, and that is the idealistic sense of purpose which I think motivates us, which is very important and a real part of American character, and has motivated a good deal of our international policy in the private church groups, in the aid groups and all the others.

Remarks to Peace Corps staff, June 14, 1962

Everything now depends upon what the government decides. Therefore, if you are interested, if you want to participate, if you feel strongly about any public question, whether it's labor, what happens in India, the future of American agriculture, whatever it may be, it seems to me that governmental service is the way to translate this interest into action.

Tape-recorded memoir entry, October 1960

For, in democracy, every citizen, regardless of his interest in politics, "holds office"; every one of us is in a position of responsibility; and, in the final analysis, the kind of government we get depends upon how we fulfill those responsibilities. We, the people, are the boss, and we will get the kind of political leadership, be it good or bad, that we demand and deserve.

Profiles in Courage, 1956

Apparently the demands of the "Cold War" are not dramatic, and thus not as well-identified, as the demands of the traditional "shooting war"— such as rationing (which we do not need), a doubling of draft quotas (which would not help) or an increase in personal income taxes (which would only impede the recovery of our economic strength).

But that does not mean that nothing is being asked of our citizens. The facts of the matter are that all the programs I am seeking—to strengthen our economy, our defenses, our image abroad, our balance of payments position and our foreign policy tools—all make demands upon one or more groups of Americans, and most often upon all Americans jointly.

All of them involve some effort, some inconvenience or some sacrifice—and, indeed, they are being opposed in some quarters on that basis.

> Letter to Alicia Patterson, editor and publisher of *Newsday*, May 16, 1961

In reaching the decision a year ago that it was imperative to build up the strength of our naval forces in a relatively short time, I was not unmindful of the many personal sacrifices a recall of our reservists would entail. However, I considered the strengthening of naval anti-submarine forces so urgent that I could find no other satisfactory alternative.

Since the recall I have been deeply impressed by the wonderful response of our naval reservists, their willing acceptance of sacrifice and their outstanding performance of duty.

> Letter to the Secretary of the Navy, July 30, 1962

Recently I heard a story of a young Peace Corpsman named Tom Scanlon who is working in Chile. He works in a village about 40 miles from an Indian village which prides itself on being communist. The village is up a long, winding road which Scanlon has gone on many occasions to see the chief. Each time the chief avoided seeing him.

Finally he saw him and said, "You are not going to talk us out of being communists." Scanlon said, "I am not trying to do that, only to talk to you about how I can help." The chief looked at him and replied, "In a few weeks the snow will come. Then you will have to park your Jeep 20 miles from here and come through 5 feet of snow on foot. The communists are willing to do that. Are you?"

When a friend saw Scanlon recently and asked him what he was doing, he said, "I am waiting for the snow."

> Remarks to governmental summer interns, June 20, 1962

This is a great country and requires a good deal of all of us, so I can imagine nothing more important than for all of you to continue to work in public affairs and be interested in them.

> Remarks to Girls Nation, August 2, 1963

The educated citizen has an obligation to serve the public. He may be a precinct worker or president. He may give his talents at the courthouse, the state house, the White House. He may be a civil servant or a senator, a candidate or a campaign worker, a winner or a loser. But he must be a participant and not a spectator.

"At the Olympic games," Aristotle wrote, "it is not the finest and strongest men who are crowned, but they who enter the lists—for out of these the prize-men are elected. So, too, in life, of the honorable and the good, it is they who act who rightly win the prizes." ...

For we can have only one form of aristocracy in this country, as Jefferson wrote long ago in rejecting John Adams' suggestion of an artificial aristocracy of wealth and birth. It is, he wrote, the natural aristocracy of character and talent, and the best form of government, he added, was that which selected these men for positions of responsibility.

> Commencement address at Vanderbilt University,
> Nashville, Tennessee, May 18, 1963

We cannot discontinue training our young men as soldiers of war, but we also want them to be ambassadors of peace.

> Speech at the Cow Palace, San Francisco,
> November 2, 1960

One of the oldest traditions [we have] in the United States has been the sense of responsibility which we have felt as a people for our less fortunate neighbors. This goes back to our earliest beginnings in Virginia and in the Massachusetts Bay Colony. I hope it is a tradition which is as alive today as it was 300 years ago.

This country has a strong tradition of individual self-reliance, but we also recognize that there are people who, through no fault of their own, need our help—children who may be sick, who may be alone, men and women who may be ill, older people who may be deserted, all the people in our community who are our neighbors and who need our help.

> Message for the United Community Campaigns of America,
> September 22, 1963

I am convinced that the pool of people in this country of ours anxious to respond to the public service is greater than it has ever been in our history.

Campaign address in San Francisco,
November 2, 1960

CHAPTER 4

Education

"Knowledge, in truth is the great sun in the firmament. Life and power are scattered with all its beams," Daniel Webster declared in 1825. Significantly, the occasion for such oration was not the founding of a new university, but the ceremonial laying of the cornerstone of the Bunker Hill Monument—a key battle site of the American Revolution. Massachusetts' Webster ranked among John Kennedy's greatest political heroes, and it is no accident that he articulated this outlook throughout his own influential life.

As congressman and senator during the Cold War, Kennedy regarded education as a vital tool to help America—and its allies—triumph over Soviet expansionism. After the Soviets launched Sputnik in October 1957, U.S. governmental leaders saw intensified science education as vital in this global conflict. "Artificial satellites will pave the way for space travel," the Soviet news agency Tass boasted to a humiliated West. If communism could defeat the American system in the latest technology, it might also triumph ideologically as well. As a senator and then president, Kennedy worried that the emerging "third world" might look to Moscow rather than Washington, D.C., for economic development. Hence, he felt an urgent need to expand education in science and technology, especially at college and postgraduate levels.

But more than many contemporaries, Kennedy also emphasized education as a weapon against poverty and unemployment. That perspective was fundamental to his New Frontier agenda. He repeatedly stressed that expanded educational opportunity for all was vital for the United States to fully realize its potential industrially, socially, militarily, and politically.

Unfortunately, international crises and congressional resistance thwarted his educational goals. It would remain for President Lyndon Johnson to press effectively for such legislation—including Head Start, the Vocational Educational Act, and the Elementary and Secondary Education Act—as central to his own Great Society program.

The Ideal of Learning

Thomas Jefferson once said to expect the people to be ignorant and free is to expect what never was and never will be.

Press conference, December 17, 1962

The human mind is our fundamental resource.

Message to Congress on education, February 20, 1961

Education is the keystone in the arch of freedom and progress. Nothing has contributed more to the enlargement of this nation's strength and opportunities than our traditional system of free, universal elementary and secondary education, coupled with the widespread availability of college education.

For the individual, the doors to the schoolhouse, to the library and to the college lead to the richest treasures of our open society, to the power of knowledge—to the wisdom, the ideals and the culture which enriches life—and to the creative, self-disciplined understanding of society needed for good citizenship in today's changing and challenging world.

For the nation, increasing the quality and availability of education is vital to both our national security and our domestic well-being. A free nation can rise no higher than the standard of excellence set in its schools and colleges. Ignorance and illiteracy, unskilled workers and school dropouts—these and other failures of our educational system breed failures in our social and economic system: delinquency, unemployment, chronic dependence, a waste of human resources, a loss of productive power and purchasing power and an increase in tax-supported benefits.

> Message to Congress, January 29, 1963

A democracy—a country today is only as strong as its citizens are educated.

> Address at the Jefferson-Jackson Dinner, Milwaukee,
> May 12, 1962

The pursuit of knowledge implies a world where [people] are free to follow out the logic of their own ideas. It implies a world where nations are free to solve their own problems and to realize their own ideals. It implies, in short, a world where collaboration emerges [and which] is emerging before our eyes.

> Address at the University of California at Berkeley,
> March 23, 1962

Your influence is not in bombs or wealth or national fame; nor is it dependent upon political parties, pressure groups or sheer force of numbers. But the fact remains that you and your associates in the teaching profession will in the long run have more to say about the future of this country and the world than any of these—not on the battlefield, not in the council room, but in the classroom.

> Address at the Maryland State Teachers' Association,
> October 10, 1957

Knowledge is power, more so today than ever before.

> Address at the 90th Anniversary Convocation of Vanderbilt
> University, Nashville, Tennessee, May 18, 1963

Only an America which has fully educated its citizens is fully capable of tackling the complex problems and perceiving the hidden dangers of the world in which we live.

> Address intended for the Trade Mart,
> Dallas, Texas, November 22, 1963

When we neglect education, we neglect the nation.
> Address at Courthouse Square, Eugene, Oregon,
> September 7, 1960

Educational Policy Making

Everyone is for education, but they're all for a different education bill.
> Press conference, August 30, 1961

The concept that every American deserves the opportunity to attain the highest level of education of which he is capable is not new to this administration—it is a traditional ideal of democracy. But it is time that we moved toward the fulfillment of this ideal with more vigor and less delay.
> Message to Congress on education, February 6, 1962

I think the federal government has a very great responsibility in the field of education. We can't maintain our strength industrially, militarily, scientifically, or socially without very well-educated citizenry.
> Broadcast interview, "After Two Years—a Conversation with
> the President," December 17, 1962

Elementary and secondary schools are the foundation of our educational system. There is little value in our efforts to broaden and improve our higher education, or increase our supply of such skills as science and engineering, without a greater effort for excellence at this basic level of education. With our mobile population and demanding needs, this is not a matter of local or state action alone—this is a national concern.
> Message from the President, February 6, 1962

For mere money alone is not enough.... Our goal—our objective in obtaining these funds—is not simply to provide an adequate educational system—or even a merely good educational system. Our goal must be an educational system that will permit the maximum development of the talents of every American boy and girl.
> Message to the National Education Association, June 25, 1961

It is a matter of great interest that there has been an intimate relationship between the great political leaders of our country and our colleges and universities.

This university bears the name of George Washington, which showed his understanding in his day of the necessity of a free society to produce educated men and women. John Adams and John Quincy Adams from my own state of Massachusetts had an intimate relationship with Harvard University. Washington and Lee shows an intimate relationship for General (Robert E.) Lee, the fact that he was willing to devote his life at the end of the (Civil) War to educating the men and women of the South, indicated his understanding of this basic precept. Woodrow Wilson, Theodore Roosevelt—and all the rest.

Remarks at George Washington University, May 3, 1961

Learned men have been talking here of the knowledge explosion, and in all that they have said I am sure they have implied the heavy present responsibilities of institutions like this one. Yet today I want to say a word on the same theme, to impress upon you as urgently as I can the growing and insistent importance of universities in our national life.

I speak of universities because that is what Boston College has long since become. But most of what I say applies to liberal arts colleges as well. My theme is not limited to any one class of universities, public or private, religious or secular. Our national tradition of variety in higher education shows no signs of weakening, and it remains the task of each of our institutions to shape its own role among its differing sisters....

From the office that I hold, in any case, there can be no doubt today of the growing meaning of universities in America.... It is for this reason that I urge upon everyone here and in this country the pressing need for national attention and a national decision in the national interest upon the national question of education.

Address at the Boston College Centennial Ceremonies,
Newton, Massachusetts, April 20, 1963

To you, the young people who have not completed your education—who may have dropped out of school—and to those who are considering doing so—go back to your school desks when your school term begins.

Go back with a real desire to learn. Go back with an intent and purpose that will make you a better student. Go back and become prepared, so when your time comes to enter the labor force, you will be a more valuable asset to our nation.

Labor Day message to the youth of the nation, September 3, 1962

We live in an age of rapid social change and unprecedented increase of new knowledge and scientific invention. In such an age we must do all in our power to strengthen our great system of formal education. But we must not stop there. We must also recognize that a free society today demands that we keep on learning or face the threat of national deterioration.

We must educate people today for a future in which the choices to be faced cannot be anticipated by even the wisest now among us. We are on the frontier of an era which holds the possibilities of a new Golden Age in which the inroads of poverty, hunger and disease will be lessened, in which through the extension of educational opportunities, men and women everywhere will have it within their power to develop their potential capacities to the maximum.

Statement to the Adult Education Association, Denver, October 14, 1960

For our universities have become the research and training centers on which American defense and industry and agriculture and the professions depend. Our progress in all these fields depends upon a constant flow of high-caliber and skilled manpower, upon new ideas and creative applications of old ideas, upon the acquisition of skills and ability to apply those skills. Thus, today, the university is, in the words of Woodrow Wilson, "the root of our intellectual life as a nation."

And our universities are not only essential to a strong society here at home, [but] they are vital to the cause of freedom throughout the world.

Our universities are our hope for success in the intense and serious competition for supremacy in ideas, in military technology, in space, in science and all the rest in which we are now engaged with the Soviet

Union. Other nations will look to us for leadership; our prestige will rise only if we are a vital and progressing society.

And, today, the basis of vitality and progress is the trained capacity of the human mind.

Speech at Commack Arena, Commack, New York, November 6, 1960

We depend on education.... Research opens up wide horizons, and if we believe in a free society, we believe in the ability of people to make an intelligent judgment, the great mass of the people. They can't do that without the best education, and they can't get the best education without the best teachers.

Remarks to Fulbright-Hays exchange teachers, August 23, 1963

The economic impact of this lack of schooling is often chronic unemployment, dependency or delinquency, with all the consequences this entails for these individuals, their families, their communities and the nation. The twin tragedies of illiteracy and dependency are often passed on from generation to generation.

Message to Congress on education, February 6, 1962

In all the years of our national life, the American people, in partnership with their governments, have continued to insist that "the means of education shall forever be encouraged," as the Continental Congress affirmed in the Northwest Ordinance. Fundamentally, education is and must always be a local responsibility, for it thrives best when nurtured at the grassroots of our democracy.

But in our present era of economic expansion, population growth and technological advance, state, local and private efforts are insufficient. These efforts must be reinforced by national support if American education is to yield a maximum of individual development and national well-being.

Message to Congress on education, January 29, 1963

The first question, and the most important—does every American boy and girl have an opportunity to develop whatever talents they have? All of us do not have equal talent, but all of us should have an equal opportunity to develop those talents.

Commencement address at San Diego State College,
June 6, 1963

It is a fact that in my own country in the American Revolution, that revolution and the society developed thereafter was built by some of the most distinguished scholars in the history of the United States who were, at the same time, among our foremost politicians. They did not believe that knowledge was merely for the study, but they thought it was for the marketplace as well.

Address at the Free University, Berlin, Germany, June 26, 1963

Nothing distresses me more as a citizen of this country than to realize that before this decade is out, there will be eight or nine million American children who will drop out of school before they have graduated, who will go out looking for work with almost no skills to offer, at a very time when machines are taking the place of men.

What chance does a boy or girl with a sixth, seventh or eighth or ninth grade education have? What do they have to offer?

Therefore, they will live on the marginal edge of hardship and distress and poverty. They will bring up their children in that atmosphere and their children will be penalized.

So we ought to keep our children in school and we ought to make them work.

Remarks at the Las Vegas Convention Center,
September 28, 1963

Some people feel the federal government should play no role, and yet the federal government, since the land grant act and back to the Northwest Ordinance, has played a major role. I think the federal government has a great responsibility in the field of education.

We cannot maintain our strength industrially, militarily, scientifically, socially, without very well-educated citizenry.

Broadcast interview, "After Two Years—a Conversation with
the President," December 17, 1962

A boy or a girl has only a limited time in their life in which to get an education, and yet it will shape their whole lives and the lives of their children. So I am asking all American parents to urge their children to go back to school in September, to assist them in every way to stay in school. I am asking school principals, clergymen, trade union leaders, business leaders, everyone in this country to concern themselves. Here is something that all of us can do in a practical way.

Press conference, August 1, 1963

I again have been reminded that we do not have an office in the government which concerns itself solely with the guidance and welfare of some 50,000 foreign students in this country.... This is a serious shortcoming on our part and one that should be remedied as swiftly as possible.... I feel very strongly that we must not allow these students—especially the Africans and Asians—to leave this country disappointed any longer.

Memo to the Secretary of State Dean Rusk, August 8, 1961

No medical school serves a purely local function. Its student body comes from all parts of the country and from every racial and religious group. Its faculty has been recruited from leading universities, medical schools and hospital centers in different parts of the country. Its graduates will go on to serve far flung communities, in all branches of medicine. Some will become general practitioners—who are the backbone of American medicine; some will become specialists; some will become teachers, who in turn, will train other students for medical careers. Many will go into research and contribute their talents and skills toward the conquest of disease and the prolonging of human life.

Address marking the opening of the Albert Einstein
College of Medicine, Bronx, New York, October 17, 1955

The problem of raising school standards has had such broad and critical implications for our national survival that we ought to have all the people we can giving it their intelligence, and indeed prayerful consideration, whether in state, local or national groups.

Interview with *New York Herald Tribune*, September 25, 1960

CHAPTER 5

Promoting Health and Social Well-Being

"I see one-third of a nation ill-housed, ill-clad, and ill-nourished" President Franklin D. Roosevelt declared in his 1937 inaugural address. Not only was this sentiment the foundation for considerable New Deal legislation, but it remained a moral imperative that motivated John Kennedy throughout his political career. As senator in the 1950s, he fought for programs to provide housing, medical care, and recreational facilities for older Americans, as well as hospital, nursing, and medical care. Although Kennedy's New Frontier inaugural address focused solely on urgent international issues like the Cold War arms race, his administration sought strong governmental action on these domestic concerns.

A particular impetus among Kennedy's circle for battling on this front came with the publication of Michael Harrington's landmark book, *The Other America*, in 1962. "Clothes make the poor invisible," its author caustically wrote. "America has the best-dressed poverty the world has ever known."

Embracing Harrington's viewpoint, Kennedy in frequent news conferences and public speeches called for federal aid to support job training, better housing, literacy programs, and services for the elderly. To overcome the growing problems of juvenile delinquency through governmental action was another social issue he often emphasized.

But faced with a sluggish economy and a slow-moving Congress, Kennedy accomplished little in this domain. Rather, after his death it remained for his vice president, Lyndon Johnson, to push New Frontier proposals vigorously in what he termed a "war on poverty." Expanding these into his Great Society program, Johnson won passage of Medicare, the Job Corps, VISTA, and other initiatives to enhance Americans' social well-being.

Eliminating Poverty at Home and Abroad

I shall never forget what I have seen. I have seen men, proud men, looking for work who cannot find it. I have seen people over 40 who are told that their services are no longer needed—too old. I have seen young people who want to live in the state, forced to leave the state for opportunities elsewhere,…I have seen unemployed miners and their families eating a diet of dry rations.
Campaign speech in West Virginia, April 1960

The United States and a few other fortunate nations are part of an island of prosperity in a worldwide sea of poverty. Our affluence has at times stricken us from the great poverty-stricken majority of the world's people.
Letter to Congress on strengthening the Peace Corps, July 4, 1963

The country cannot continue to expect a steady rise in our national growth rate unless these areas of the United States which have been islands of poverty in many cases and islands of distress in nearly every case in the last decade are dealt with.
Address to the Northern Great Lakes Region Land and People
Conference, Duluth, Minnesota, September 24, 1963

The problems of government are becoming more and more complex, and the relationships between state and federal government more and more interdependent.

We are all engaged, both in the state and federal levels and the local level, in a common effort to reduce unemployment, and to eliminate poverty among our people; to make our urban centers a better place in which to live; to guarantee equal opportunity in all fields; to conquer mental retardation and mental illness; to keep this country strong, to keep it in a position where it can fulfill its responsibilities to all the free world.

> Remarks to the National Conference of State Legislative Leaders, September 21, 1963

For the blessings of life have not been distributed evenly to the Family of Man. Life expectancy in this most fortunate of nations has reached the Biblical three score years and ten; but in the less developed nations of Africa, Asia and Latin America, the overwhelming majority of infants cannot expect to live even two score years and five. In those vast continents, more than half of the children of primary school age are not in school. More than half the families live in substandard dwellings....

The Family of Man can survive differences of race and religion....It can accept differences of ideology, politics and economics. But it cannot survive, in the form in which we know it, a nuclear war—and neither can it long endure the growing gulf between the rich and the poor.

The rich must help the poor. The industrialized nations must help the developing nations.

> Speech to the Protestant Council of the City of New York, November 8, 1963

Overcoming the Problems of Young Americans

I have received reports indicating that there has been an increase in the amount of juvenile delinquency in both urban and rural communities. This delinquency seems to occur most often among school drop-outs and unemployed youth faced with limited opportunities and from broken families.

I view the present trend with serious concern. Juvenile delinquency and youth offenses diminish the strength and the vitality of our nation. They present serious problems to all the communities affected, and they leave indelible impressions upon the people involved which often cause continuing problems.

> Letter to Congress concerning measures to
> combat juvenile delinquency, May 11, 1961

Now, I feel that we are a city on a hill and that one of our great responsibilities during these days is to make sure that we in this country set an example to the world not only of helping and assisting them to fulfill their own destiny, but also demonstrating what a free people can do.

We cannot possibly permit, therefore, the waste of hundreds and thousands of young boys and girls who grow up in underprivileged areas, many of them in our northern cities, ignored in many cases by their families and their community who drift into life without hope of ever developing their talents and who ultimately may end up, as so many do, in a life of crime when they're young, which stains their life from then on.

> Remarks to Big Brothers of America, June 7, 1961

I saw cases in West Virginia, here in the United States, where children took home part of their school lunch in order to feed their families, because I don't think we are meeting our obligations toward these Americans.

> Opening statement in debate with Richard Nixon,
> Chicago, September 26, 1960

No nation can neglect the development of its young people without courting catastrophe....

We are apathetic toward the defeatism, born of social and economic "exile," that afflicts the hearts and minds of many modern slum dwellers, and the cynical attitude this produces in slum youth.

We are permitting many of our talented young workers to be relegated to menial jobs, or to stark unemployment, merely because of the accident of race.

> Statement on youth employment, April 24, 1963

Promoting Housing and Urban Affairs

Housing goes to the very basic life of the family and we are anxious to make sure that every American has a chance to live as he chooses and to bring up his family the way he wants.

> Remarks on searing in David Lawrence to the President's Committee on Equal Opportunity, February 1, 1963

It is the ambition of this administration to try to provide decent housing for all American families.

> Remarks on swearing in the Housing and Home Finance administrator, February 11, 1961

In a few short decades we have passed from a rural to an urban way of life; in a few short decades more, we shall be a nation of vastly expanded population, living in expanded urban areas in housing that does not now exist, served by community facilities that do not now exist, moving about by means of systems of urban transportation that do not now exist.

The challenge is great, and the time is short.

> Message to Congress, January 30, 1962

A nation that is partly ill-housed is not as strong as a nation with adequate homes for every family. A nation with ugly, crime-infested cities and haphazard suburbs does not present the same image to the world as a nation characterized by bright and orderly urban development.

> Message to Congress on housing and community development, March 9, 1961

A strong America depends on its cities—America's glory, and sometimes America's shame.

> State of the Union Address, January 11, 1962

Safeguarding Health

The health of our people is our nation's most precious resource.
> Address marking the opening of the Albert Einstein College of
> Medicine, Bronx, New York, October 17, 1955

Our efforts to protect the American people against unsafe and worthless drug products is a source of great concern to us all.
> Letter to Congress on the need for safer drugs, August 5, 1962

American doctors and medical facilities are the finest in the world and research and application of new discoveries almost daily broadens the horizon of hope—yet the cost of medical care is too often prohibitive for those who need it most, our elderly population living on limited incomes.
> Labor Day statement, September 3, 1962

The future health of our nation rests on the care of our children and the development of our knowledge of the medical and biological sciences.
> Statement on bill authorizing a National Institute of Child Health
> and Human Development, October 17, 1962

What I think we are all concerned about is that children have a happy childhood, and a fruitful one, and that adults be permitted to work and that older people find their later years to be easier, free from pain and discomfort.
> Interview with Dave Garroway for the *Today* show,
> January 31, 1961

We can take justifiable pride in our achievements in the field of medicine. We stand among the select company of nations for whom fear of the great epidemic plagues is long past. Our life expectancy has already reached the biblical three score and ten, and unlike so many less fortunate peoples of the world, we need not struggle for mere survival.
But measured against our capacity and capability in the fields of

health and medical care, measured against the scope of the problems that remain and the opportunities to be seized, this nation still falls far short of its responsibility.

> Message to Congress on national health needs, February 27, 1962

But I do think it is fair to say that in the field of mental retardation we have been behind.

> Remarks to the National Association for Retarded Children, October 24, 1963

Few nations do more than the United States to assist their least fortunate citizens—to make certain that no child, no elderly or handicapped citizen, no family in any circumstances in any state is left without the essential needs for a decent and healthy existence.

In too few nations, I might add, are the people aware of the progressive strides this country has taken in demonstrating the humanitarian side of freedom.

> Message to Congress on public welfare programs, February 1, 1962

Society for too long has closed the door against the mentally retarded. Too often too many have been hidden in attics, locked up in institutions and neglected in their communities....

We have, in the past, forfeited a unique opportunity to develop an otherwise wasted human resource....

Never in the history of man has it been possible to achieve greater gains against this grave and complex problem. Recently acquired medical and scientific knowledge now make it possible to assure a productive and self-respecting life for the great majority of the mentally retarded.

> Letter at the White House Conference on Mental Retardation, September 19, 1963

Really, any childhood sickness is bound to affect any adult, but any childhood sickness which goes on through life, without any hope of recovery, is bound to be the most deadly of all burdens which any person must carry and which their families must carry.

> Remarks to the Joseph P. Kennedy Foundation, December 6, 1962

Most of the major diseases of the body are beginning to give ground in man's increasing struggle to find their cause and cure. But the public understanding, treatment and prevention of mental disabilities have not made comparable progress since the earliest days of modern history.

Yet mental illness and mental retardation are among our most critical health problems. They occur more frequently, affect more people, require more prolonged treatment, cause more suffering by the families of the afflicted, waste more of our human resources, and constitute more financial drain upon both the public treasury and the personal finances of the individual families than any other single condition.

> Message to Congress on mental illness and mental retardation,
> February 5, 1963

Mental retardation ranks with mental health as a major health, social and economic problem in this country. It strikes our most precious asset, our children. It disables ten times as many people as diabetes, thirty times as many as tuberculosis and 600 times as many as infantile paralysis.

> Remarks on measures to combat mental illness and
> mental retardation, February 5, 1963

The vigor of our country, its physical vigor and energy, is going to be no more advanced, no more substantial, than the vitality and will of our countrymen....

I think during this period we should make every effort to see that the intellectual talents of every boy and girl are developed to the maximum. And that also their physical fitness, their willingness to participate in physical exercise, their willingness to participate in physical contests, in athletic contests—all these, I think, will do a good deal to strengthen this country, and also to contribute to a greater enjoyment of life in the years to come.

> Remarks on the Youth Fitness program, July 19, 1961

The manner in which our nation cares for its citizens and conserves its manpower resources is more than an index to its concern for the less fortunate. It is a key to its future.

> Statement on a national program to combat mental retardation,
> October 11, 1961

The intensive medical research effort begun shortly after World War II is now showing dramatic results. The array of modern drugs, appliances and techniques available to prevent and cure disease is impressive in scope and in quality.

But each improvement raises our horizons. Each success enables us to concentrate more on the remaining dangers, and on new challenges and threats to health. Some of these new challenges result from our changing environment, some from our new habits and activities....

More people are living in huge metropolitan and industrial complexes, where they face a host of new problems in achieving safety even in the common environmental elements of food, water, land and air. The hazards of modern living also raise new problems of psychological stability.

> Message to Congress on improving the nation's health,
> February 7, 1963

Enhancing Social Well-Being

A medical revolution has extended the life of our elder citizens without providing the dignity and security those later years deserve.

> Democratic nomination acceptance speech, Los Angeles,
> July 15, 1960

The needs of children should not be made to wait.

> Message to Congress on the nation's youth, February 14, 1963

We can no longer tolerate growing patches of poverty and injustice in America—substandard wages, unemployment, city slums, inadequate medical care, inferior education and the sad plight of migratory workers.

> Senate speech, August 10, 1960

Our concern is a better life for all Americans.

> Campaign remarks, Billings, Montana, September 22, 1960

CHAPTER 6

Labor, Employment, and Business

Born into wealth and privilege, John Kennedy never had to worry person-ally about wages or earning a living at all. But initially as a representative, and then as a member of the Senate Education and Labor Committee, he gained a reputation as moderately pro-labor while actively combating union racketeering. For example, Kennedy wrote his own report opposing the Taft-Hartley Act passed in 1947—denounced by President Truman as a "slave-labor bill" for such provisions as prohibiting unions from contributing to political campaigns.

During the 1950s, Kennedy helped lead hard-hitting efforts alongside Barry Goldwater and Joe McCarthy on the Senate's Select Committee on Labor to purge the Teamsters Union of corrupt officials including its vice president, Jimmy Hoffa, popular among many rank-and-file workers for the economic success he had brought them. As a result, many labor activists generally viewed Kennedy warily and supported his rivals Hubert Humphrey and Adlai Stevenson instead in the 1960 Democratic primaries.

It is easy to see how Kennedy positioned himself after winning his party's nomination. In a section titled "Champion of Labor," his campaign brochure noted some of his achievements such as a higher minimum wage, increased unemployment compensation, a broader federal housing program, and safer working conditions. It also noted that as "sponsor of the AFL-CIO backed anti-racketeering bill clearing labor's name of hoodlum infiltration, he succeeded in conference committee in eliminating 15 major provisions restricting honest unions—while preserving curbs on racketeers."

During his administration, Kennedy was up against a congressional coalition of southern Democrats and Republicans who hindered his legislative agenda. Nevertheless, Congress did raise the minimum wage and added 3.6 million more workers who were eligible for it. To the delight of organized labor, he appointed Arthur Goldberg, special counsel to the AFL-CIO (which boasted over 50 million union members in the 1950s), as secretary of labor. Under Kennedy's impetus, Goldberg helped mediate many labor–management disputes in major industries and fought vigorously for the rights of minority workers.

This administration harbors no ill will against any individual, any industry, corporation or segment of the American economy. Our goals of economic growth and price stability are dependent upon the success of both corporations, business and labor and there can be no room on either side in this country at this time for any feelings of hostility or vindictiveness.

When a mistake has been retracted and the public interest preserved, nothing is to be gained from further public recrimination.

Press conference, April 18, 1962

When I read some of those great editorials about labor, I like to think about how it is to go to work at 6 o'clock in the morning at zero degrees.

Address at the Jefferson-Jackson Dinner, Milwaukee, May 12, 1962

Once the free trade union movement is destroyed, once it is harnessed to the chariot of the state, once trade union leaders are nominated by the head of the state, once meetings such as this become formalities, endorsing the purposes of the state, the trade union movement is destroyed and so is democracy.

Remarks to the Trade Union Congress of German Construction
Workers, Berlin, June 26, 1963

Thus this Labor Day again makes the vital distinction between opposing ways of life in the modern world. We celebrate the labor of our people precisely because we believe it to be an essential to man's dignity, performed freely and in good conscience, and commanding by right a just reward.

We look upon man's toil as an expression of individual personality and will, not a commodity to be exploited for the benefit of a state or ruling political party. Tyranny deprives a man of the freedom and joy of his work.

These beliefs underlie our system of self-government in economic life. Our free and democratic labor movement is based upon the advancement of individual dignity.

> Labor Day statement, August 29, 1961

We cannot permit this very rich country and strong country of ours to have so many of our younger people unemployed, wandering the streets, without facilities.... There's going to be less and less need in this country, in this economy, for unskilled labor.

> Remarks on the President's Committee on Juvenile Delinquency and Youth Crime, May 31, 1962

We are going into a critical phase of our national life. We want to keep our economy free—we want labor to be free—we want management to be free—and we want to keep the federal government in its proper role.

> Remarks to the President's Advisory Committee on Labor–Management Policy, March 21, 1961

No greater service to the cause of the free world could possibly come forward than the development of effective, liberal, free trade unions in the emerging countries.... And the way progress can be made over a wide spectrum for the great majority of people is by having an effective labor movement.

> Address to the United Auto Workers, Atlantic City, New Jersey, May 8, 1962

I don't know why it is that expenditures which deal with the enforcement of the minimum wage, that deal with the problem of school dropouts, of retraining of workers, of unskilled labor, all the problems that are so much with us…, why they are always regarded as the waste in the budget, and expenditures for defense are always regarded as the untouchable item in the budget.

> Remarks on the 50th Anniversary of the Department of Labor, March 4, 1963

You cannot maintain a free society today, in my opinion, unless you have a free trade union movement, and the trade union movement is effective not only because it is a means of securing a fair share of national productivity for the men and women who labor but it is also the means of supporting a broad program of social progress.

> Remarks to Latin American and Caribbean students attending the Institute for Free Trade Union Development, August 8, 1962

Unemployment insurance by itself is not a cure for such unemployment, nor is it the only measure necessary to deal with the problem.

> Letter to Congress on strengthening the unemployment insurance system, May 14, 1963

We are a blessed land. More Americans are working than at any time in our history, earning more and producing the highest volume of goods and services on record. They enjoy economic and social protections and rights undreamed of in earlier times—and flatly denied in contemporary communist societies. Our labor organizations are free and strong, with a solid tradition of achievement.

> Labor Day statement, September 3, 1962

This is the 24th day of virtually complete shutdown of all Atlantic and Gulf Coast ports resulting from the strike by the International Longshoremen's Association.

The shutdown is doing intolerable injury to the national welfare. Hundreds of ships are immobilized. Over 100,000 longshore and maritime workers are idle. Economic losses to the nation are running at a rate of millions of dollars a day. Serious damage is being done [to] the United States dollar balance. Vital foreign aid and relief shipments are blocked. The lifeline between Puerto Rico and the mainland has been cut, and commerce imperative to the economic well-being of the free world is disrupted.

> Statement on the longshoremen's strike, January 16, 1963

And therefore I think it is a free judgment to make that a free, active, progressive trade union movement stands for a free, active, progressive country, and that is the kind of country I am proud to be president of.

> Remarks to the International Association of Machinists,
> May 5, 1963

The out-of-work college graduate is just as much out of work as a school dropout. The family beset by unemployment cannot send a child to college. It may even encourage him to drop out of high school to find a job which he will not keep.

> Remarks to the AFL-CIO, New York,
> November 15, 1963

Strikes make the headlines. Yet...over twice as much time was lost from job accidents as from strikes.

Every family whose breadwinner is struck down by one of these accidents, despite workmen's compensation and welfare and pension plans, suffers deprivation as well as heartbreak.

The nation, which is investing millions of dollars in training and retraining manpower, in enriching our skills to meet the demands of technological progress, cannot afford to waste that investment through preventable work injuries.

> Statement at conference on occupational safety, April 3, 1963

The unemployed whose skills have been rendered obsolete by automation and other technological changes must be equipped with new skills enabling them to become productive members of our society once again. The skills of other workers must also be improved to enable them to meet the more demanding requirements of modern industry.

> Letter to Congress concerning the training of workers in
> new occupational skills, May 29, 1961

The ideal of full employment, in the large sense that each individual shall become all that he is capable of becoming, and shall contribute fully to the well being of the nation even as he fully shares in that well being, is at the heart of our democratic belief. If we have never achieved that ideal, neither have we ever for long been content to fall short of it.

We have measured ourselves by the persistence of our effort to meet the standard of the full development and use of our human resources. As we still fall short of that standard, we are still not satisfied.

> Message to Congress on manpower, March 11, 1963

We cannot permit...an important segment of our population to be denied an opportunity to find decent jobs, to be the first to be unemployed and the last to be rehired, and to be at the bottom of the ladder, and regard that as an acceptable situation.

> Remarks at the signing of Equal Opportunity Agreements,
> January 17, 1963

The support that the trade union movement has historically given to our foreign policy is one of the great satisfactions and strengths of our democratic government.

> Letter to AFL-CIO president George Meany,
> June 28, 1961

Organized labor can look back on thirty years of supporting progressive causes, not only at home, which happened to benefit their members, but also around the world.

> Remarks to the United Steelworkers of America, Tampa, Florida,
> November 8, 1963

Technology and Labor

A revolution of automation finds machines replacing men in the mines and mills of America, without replacing their incomes or their training or their needs to pay the family doctor, grocer and landlord.

> Democratic nomination acceptance speech, Los Angeles, July 15, 1960

Advances in technology require a more highly skilled working force. History has shown that increases in productivity account for two-thirds of our economic growth. The rise in productivity comes from improvements in the skills of the labor force, improvements in technology, and better organization of production. In these areas, education is vital and its advancement will increase our rate of growth.

> Statement for the National Educational Association's *NEA Journal*, October 1960

The problem, of course, is that even in a period of recovery, there are these islands of unemployment which have been left behind for many years as a result of successive recessions and technological changes. And these people, with some of them the unemployment may average 10, 13, 15 percent in places like sections of northern Minnesota, Pennsylvania, West Virginia, eastern Kentucky, and southern Illinois. I think we ought to help these people.

> Press conference, March 29, 1962

It is equally clear that technology cannot be forced on a people, save by a tyranny that destroys as much as it creates. The full cooperation of workers, through their trade unions, must be achieved. This is a rule of economic development, and equally a fundamental tenet of a free society.

It is not a coincidence that wherever political democracy flourishes in the modern world there is also a strong, active, responsible free trade union movement.

> Message to the Inter-American Conference of Ministers of Labor, May 7, 1963

CHAPTER 7

Challenges to American Agriculture

Affluent, city-bred, and Ivy League-educated, Kennedy learned much about agricultural politics and policy during his years in Congress. As he traveled the campaign trail toward the White House, American agriculture was struggling with crippling problems such as farm failures, recession, and declining farm income. He knew that the health of the industry was a key indicator of the health of the national economy.

As president, Kennedy repeatedly cited interconnections between the economic stability of American farmers, foreign aid, international trade, and hunger at home and abroad. Even so, it was a realm fraught with political minefields as he faced such controversies as paying subsidies to farmers, sending surplus food to communist China, and creating a food stamp program. During his tenure, Kennedy wrestled with problems concerning the government's stockpile of surplus grain, rural poverty, substandard housing, vocational training, and promotion of exports of farm products. Underlying the administration's development of legislative policies was Kennedy's awareness that farmers still carried significant influence at the polls and that garnering the support of farm-state members of Congress was thus politically vital.

66

The Role of American Agriculture

As long as there are hungry families—mothers, fathers and children—throughout the world, we cannot possibly believe or feel that our great agricultural production, in any sense, is a burden. It is a great asset, not only for ourselves but for people all over the world; and I think that instead of using the term "surpluses" and regarding it, in a sense, as a failure, we should regard it as one of the great evidences of our country's capacity, and also as a great resource, in order to demonstrate our concern for our fellow man.

Remarks for the United Nations Freedom from Hunger campaign, November 22, 1961

In July 1862, in the darkest days of the Civil War, President Abraham Lincoln signed two acts which were to help to mold the future of the nation which he was then struggling to preserve.

The first of these, the Homestead Act, provided, in Carl Sandburg's words, "a farm free to any man who wanted to put a plow into unbroken sod."

The second, the Morrill Act, donated more than one million acres of federal land to endow at least one university in every state of the Union.

Thus, even as the nation trembled on the brink of destruction, the vast lands of the American West were open to final settlement. A new America of unparalleled abundance began to grow.

Message for the centennial convocation of the Association of Land-Grant Colleges and State Universities, November 12, 1961

This is really a most outstanding accomplishment of our civilization in this century, to produce more food with less people than any country on earth.

Remarks on signing the Agricultural Act, August 8, 1961

Under the American system of agriculture, our farmers produce an abundance which is a marvelous technical achievement, and at the same time a mighty weapon in the war against hunger.

The United States has used this abundance to combat hunger abroad, and to provide nations striving to develop their economies with the means of improving the health and vigor of their citizens.

> Statement on signing the World Food Congress bill,
> October 19, 1962

For there is a close relationship between prosperity on the farm and prosperity in the city—between the economic health of our farm community and the economic health of our nation.

> Remarks to the National Conference on Milk and Nutrition,
> January 23, 1962

Our Food for Peace program is increasingly using our agricultural commodities to stimulate the economic growth of developing nations and to assist in achieving other U.S. foreign policy goals.

> Message to Congress on Free World defense and assistance
> programs, April 2, 1963

Proper management of our resources of food and fiber is a key factor in the economic future of our nation....Our capacity to produce still outruns the growth of both domestic and foreign demand for food and fiber. Our abundance must be harnessed in such a way as to bring supply and demand more nearly into balance.

And the benefits of our agricultural process still need to be translated into improved income to farm families, lower prices to consumers for food and fiber, expanded exports and reduced expenditures for price support programs.

> Message to Congress on agriculture, January 31, 1963

We are today the world's largest exporter of food and fiber....In short, our farmers deserve praise, not condemnation, and their efficiency should be a cause for gratitude, not something for which they are penalized.

> Message to Congress on agriculture, March 16, 1961

American agricultural abundance offers a great opportunity for the United States to promote the interests of peace in a significant way and to play an important role in helping to provide a more adequate diet for peoples all around the world. We must make the most vigorous and constructive use possible of this opportunity. We must narrow the gap between abundance here at home and near starvation abroad. Humanity and prudence alike counsel a major effort on our part.

> Memorandum on the Food for Peace program, January 24, 1961

So that when we talk about agriculture we should talk about it with pride and not always talk about it as one of our great problems or burdens. It is, really, one of the great success stories of the United States— and of the whole free world.

> Remarks to State Agricultural Stabilization and Conservation committees, April 4, 1962

Obstacles Facing Agriculture

The neglected educational needs of America's one million migrant agricultural workers and their families constitute one of the gravest reproaches to our nation. The interstate and seasonal movement of migrants imposes severe burdens on those school districts which have the responsibility for providing education to those who live there temporarily.

> Message to Congress on education, February 6, 1962

Almost a fifth of the occupied houses in the rural areas of America are so dilapidated that they must be replaced. Hundreds of thousands of other rural homes are far below the level of comfort and convenience considered adequate in our nation.

> Special Message to Congress on housing and community development, March 9, 1961

A technological revolution on the farm has led to an output explosion— but we have not yet learned to harness that explosion usefully, while protecting our farmers' right to full parity income.

> Democratic nomination acceptance speech, Los Angeles, July 15, 1960

Our agricultural problems and opportunities are different from those of much of the world. We have a tremendous capacity to produce, which has really been the most extraordinary revolution, really, in a sense of a kind that we have had in the last fifteen years. In other countries their problem has been different: an inadequacy of supply.

So how we shall maintain our production, how we shall improve our consumption, how we shall maintain the income of our farmers, how we shall take care of those who no longer are needed to produce our food, and how other sections of the world shall be able to market their surpluses in those countries where they have them, in concert with us, in a way which serves the very basic needs of the people of the world—all that is worth your attention and effort, and in most cases your lives.

Remarks to the World Food Forum, May 17, 1962

Management of our agricultural resources to meet the triple goals of increased farm income, lower cost to the taxpayer and reduced farm surpluses continues to be one of the most difficult problems confronting the nation.

Message to Congress on agriculture, January 31, 1962

We will intensify our campaign against rural poverty and our drive to build a thriving diversified rural economy.

Special Message to Congress on agriculture, January 31, 1963

I am sorry to see the important agricultural leaders opposing giving us the protection which is required. You cannot have the federal government supporting agriculture in important ways unless there is some control over production and unless there is some limitation, some provision for cross-compliance. Otherwise, the farmers' income will continue to drop, and we will have a gradual deterioration of agriculture in this country.

Press conference, March 15, 1961

The farmer plants in the spring and harvests in the fall. There are hundreds of thousands of them. They really don't—are not able to control their market very well. They bring their crops in or their livestock in, many of them, about the same time. They have only a few purchasers that buy their milk or their hogs, a few large companies, in many cases, and, therefore, the farmer is not in a position to bargain very effectively in the marketplace.

I think the experience of the '20s has shown what a free market could do to agriculture. And if the agricultural economy collapses, then the economy of the rest of the United States sooner or later will collapse.

The farmers are the No. 1 market for the automobile industry of the United States. The automobile industry is the No. 1 market for steel. So, if the farmers' economy continues to decline as sharply as it has in recent years, then I think you would have a recession in the rest of the country. So I think the case for the government intervention is a good one.

> Debate with Vice President Richard Nixon, Chicago,
> September 26, 1960

In many rural areas, the difficulty of financing adequate safe and sanitary housing and modern community facilities such as water and sewage systems, recreational installations and transportation has deterred general community improvement and more rapid industrialization.

> Special Message to Congress on agriculture, January 31, 1962

The marginal or displaced farmer is most painfully aware of the interdependence of agriculture and industry.

> Message to Congress on economic recovery and growth,
> February 2, 1961

In regard to the effect of automation on agriculture...I know this problem is a matter of substantial concern to all of us. Some of our most serious problems have arisen because of research combined with automation, which have brought an extraordinary increase in production, with far less manpower. Agriculture, where we have a great increase in production, with around four million people less than we had several years ago, in many ways is one of the most extraordinary and admirable facets of our national life.

I think it is unfortunate that we are not yet able to bring it more to the attention of the world, where so many people, including in the Soviet Union and China, are spending most of their time on subsistence agriculture, that we are able to have this extraordinary production with very few people. But like all blessings, they bring problems with them.

Press conference, April 21, 1961

CHAPTER 8

Environment and Natural Resources

John Kennedy had a recreational interest in the outdoors and favored protection of public lands from overuse. At times, he demonstrated great foresight, as in his warnings about what we today call urban sprawl and suburban sprawl—and in his call to preserve open spaces. The sea also exerted a near-mystical hold on the President, perhaps because of his family home on Cape Cod, Massachusetts, his love of boating, and his South Pacific naval exploits during World War II. He thus envisioned the oceans as a bounteous frontier.

Like many members of his generation, the power of science and the promise of exploration lured Kennedy. He believed that those twin engines of the human mind and spirit could solve societal problems without environmental damage. Thus his calls emerged to develop solar energy, for example, and to make the deserts bloom. Overall, however, Kennedy's legislative initiatives reflected a policy that environmental interests should not trump the needs of agriculture and economic development, and that natural resources such as energy and water should be exploitable.

To place these matters in a political context, Kennedy recognized that the increasing political influence of the western states came largely from the economic growth that resulted from gas and oil drilling there. And as the population expanded in the American West, there would correspondingly be a greater need to supply water for its farms, ranches, homes, and industries.

Protecting the Environment

If we continue to ignore the polluting of our streams, the littering of our national forests, we will be denying to ourselves and to our children a heritage which we were the beneficiaries of.

> Campaign remarks, Valley Forge, Pennsylvania, October 19, 1960

Land is the most precious resource of the metropolitan area. The present patterns of haphazard suburban development are contributing to a tragic waste in the use of a vital resource now being consumed at an alarming rate.

Open space must be preserved to provide parks and recreation, conserve water and other natural resources, prevent building in undesirable locations, prevent erosion and floods, and avoid the wasteful extension of public services. Open land is also needed to provide reserves for future residential development, to protect against undue speculation and to make it possible for state and regional bodies to control the rate and character of community development.

> Message to Congress on housing and community development,
> March 9, 1961

The history of America is, more than that of most nations, the history of man confronted by nature....From the beginning, Americans had a lively awareness of the land and the wilderness.

> Introduction to *The Quiet Crisis* by Stewart Udall, 1963

We depend on our natural resources to sustain us—but in turn their continued availability must depend on our using them prudently, improving them wisely and, where possible, restoring them promptly.

We must reaffirm our dedication to the sound practices of conservation which can be defined as the wise use of our natural environment. It is in the final analysis, the highest form of national thrift—the prevention of waste and despoilment while preserving, improving and renewing the quality and usefulness of all our resources.

Our deep spiritual confidence that this nation will survive the perils of today—which may well be with us for decades to come—compels us to invest in our nation's future, to consider and meet our obligations to our children and the numberless generations that will follow.

> Message to Congress on conservation, March 1, 1962

Wise investment in a resource program today will return vast dividends tomorrow, and failures to act now may be opportunities lost forever.

> Message to Congress on natural resources, February 23, 1961

We live in the midst of a population explosion that is remaking the face of America. The country is filling up, recreation areas are overcrowded, our cities are jammed, our highways are clogged, and on the edges of our great cities the shopping center and ranch house have replaced the silo and the haystack until today more than a fourth of all Americans live in suburbs.

> Speech at Meadowdale Shopping Center, Carpentersville, Illinois,
> October 25, 1960

You cannot possibly move ahead in this country, we cannot possibly develop our resources, we cannot possibly develop our strength unless we make the best use we can of the land, the water, the minerals that have been given to us and which have made our country great.

> Campaign remarks, Saginaw, Michigan, October 14, 1960

Good urban transportation can shape as well as serve urban growth.

> Letter to Congress on transportation needs of the
> Washington, D.C., Area, May 27, 1963

I really don't know why it is that all of us are so committed to the sea, except I think it's because in addition to the fact that the sea changes, and the light changes and ships change, it's because we all came from the sea. And it is an interesting biological fact that all of us have, in our veins, the exact same percentage of salt in our blood that exists in the ocean and, therefore, we have salt in our blood, in our sweat, in our tears. We are tied to the ocean. And when we go back to the sea—whether it is to sail or to watch it—we are going back from whence we came.

Remarks at a dinner for the America's Cup crew,
Newport, Rhode Island, September 14, 1962

Throughout our history, our soil and water, our forests and minerals, have provided the resources upon which this country grew—and our power ascended. Today, this great gift of material wealth provides the foundation upon which the defense of freedom rests, here and around the world. And our future greatness and our strength depend upon the continued abundant use of our natural resources.

Thus it is our task in our time and in our generation to hand down undiminished to those who come after us, as was handed down to us by those who went before, the natural wealth and beauty which is ours. To do this will require constant attention and vigilance—sustained vigor and imagination.

Remarks at the National Wildlife Federation, March 3, 1961

There are two points on conservation that have come home to me in the last two days. One is the necessity for us to protect what we already have, what nature gave to us, and use it well, not to waste water or land, to set aside land and water, recreation, wilderness and all the rest now so that it will be available to those who come in the future. That is the traditional concept of conservation, and it still has a major part in the life of the United States.

But the other part of conservation is the newer part, and that is to use science and technology to achieve significant breakthroughs as we are doing today, and in that way to conserve the resources which ten or twenty or thirty years ago may have been totally unknown. So we use nuclear power for peaceful purposes and power. We use new techniques to develop new kinds of coal and oil from shale, and all the rest. We use new techniques...in oceanography, so from the bottom of the ocean and the ocean we get all the resources which are there, and which are going to be mined and harvested. And from the sun we are going to find more and more uses for that energy whose power we are so conscious of today.

Remarks at the Hanford Electric Generating Plant,
Hanford, Washington, September 26, 1963

One of the great resources which we are going to find in the next forty years is not going to be the land—it will be the ocean. We are going to find untold wealth in the oceans of the world which will be used to make a better life for our people.

Science is changing all of our natural environment. It can change it for good; it can change it for bad. We are pursuing, for example, new opportunities in coal, which have been largely neglected—examining the feasibility of transporting coal by water through pipelines, of gasification at the mines, of liquefaction of coal into gasoline and of transmitting electric power directly from the mouth of the mine....At the same time, we are engaged in active research on better means of using low-grade coal to meet the tremendous increase in the demand for coal we are going to find in the rest of this century.

This is, in effect, using science to increase our supply of a resource of which the people of the United States were totally unaware fifty years ago.

Address at the University of Wyoming, Cheyenne,
September 25, 1963

Every time we make a determination to set aside a seashore for the use of future generations, every time we build these great projects, we develop the water resources, we set aside recreational areas, we can be sure they are going to be used.

Remarks at the dedication of the Whiskeytown Dam and
Reservoir, Shasta County, California, September 28, 1963

In the light of the known damage caused by polluted air, both to our health and to our economy, it is imperative that greater emphasis be given to the control of air pollution by communities, states and the federal government....

The long-range assault of multiple environmental contaminations on human health are cumulative and interrelated. It is of great importance, therefore, that our efforts to learn about and control health hazards be unified and mutually supporting.

> Message to Congress on improving the nation's health,
> February 7, 1963

The nation needs a land acquisition program to preserve both prime federal and state areas for outdoor recreation purposes. The growth of our cities, the development of our industry, the expansion of our transportation systems—all manifestations of our vigorous and expanding society—preempt irreplaceable lands of natural beauty and unique recreation value.

In addition to the enhancement of spiritual, cultural and physical values resulting from the preservation of these resources, the expenditures for their preservation are a sound financial investment.

> Letter to Congress on outdoor recreation needs,
> February 14, 1963

The provision of adequate outdoor recreational opportunities for our growing population continues to be a pressing problem.

> Budget Message to Congress, January 17, 1963

I would suggest...a worldwide program to protect land and water, forests and wildlife; to combat exhaustion and erosion; to stop the contamination of water and air by industrial as well as nuclear pollution; and to provide for the steady renewal and expansion of the natural bases of life.

> Address at the National Academy of Sciences, October 22, 1963

It is obvious that unless international conservation agreements are strictly enforced, there is a grave danger of permanent injury to our ocean resources.

> Statement on the North Pacific fisheries negotiations,
> September 10, 1963

Have we ever thought why such a small proportion of our beaches should be available for public use, how it is that so many of our great cities have been developed without parks or playgrounds, why so many of our rivers are so polluted, why the air we breathe is so impure or why the erosion of our land was permitted to run so large?

I think there is evidence, however, that this nation can take action—action for which those who come after us will be grateful, which will convert killers and spoilers into allies—by building dams for many purposes, by state and local and national parks, by developing the productivity of our farms, reclaiming land, preventing soil from washing away.

> Address at the Pinchot Institute for Conservation Studies, Milford, Pennsylvania, September 24, 1963

If promptly developed, recreational activities and new national park, forest and recreation areas can bolster your economy and provide pleasure for millions of people in the days to come....

The precise manner in which these resources are used, land and water, is of the greatest importance. There is need for comprehensive local, state, regional and national planning.

> Remarks on arrival at the airport, Ashland, Wisconsin, September 24, 1963

In the field of conservation, every day that is lost is a valuable opportunity wasted.

> Remarks at the University of North Dakota, Grand Forks, September 25, 1963

Using Natural Resources

Knowledge of the oceans is more than a matter of curiosity. Our very survival may hinge upon it.... To predict, and perhaps some day to control, changes in weather and climate is of the utmost importance to man everywhere. These changes are controlled to a large and yet unknown extent by what happens in the ocean. Ocean and atmosphere work together in a still mysterious way to determine our climate.

> Letter to Congress on oceanographic research, March 29, 1963

The other is the natural resource of our country, particularly the land west of the 100th parallel, where the rain comes fifteen or twenty inches a year. This state [Utah] knows that the control of water is the secret of development of the West, and whether we use it for power or for irrigation or for whatever purpose, no drop of water west of the 100th parallel should flow to the ocean without being used.

> Address at the Mormon Tabernacle, Salt Lake City,
> September 26, 1963

When we think of such a large percentage of the world's land which supports so few people, how extraordinary an accomplishment it will be when we can bring water to bear on the deserts surrounding the Mediterranean and the Indian Sea and all the rest. And I think it is within our grasp and within our lifetime, perhaps even within our decade. And I think it will be the prime accomplishment of science in improving the life of people in the long history of the world.

> Remarks at White House Conference on Conservation,
> May 25, 1962

Water—one of the most familiar and abundant compounds on the earth's surface—is rapidly becoming a limiting factor on further economic growth in many areas of this nation and the world. As time goes on, more communities will be faced with the prospect of economic distress and stagnation unless alternative sources of suitable water are developed.

> Letter to Congress on saline water research, June 26, 1961

The economic growth of the United States has been favored by the abundant supply of natural resources of almost every sort. But resource needs and supplies are not static. As our needs mount, as past reserves are depleted and as technological requirements change, we must constantly develop new supplies if growth is not to be inhibited.

> Message to Congress on economic recovery and growth,
> February 2, 1961

Our primary task now is to increase our understanding of our environment, to a point where we can enjoy it without defacing it, use its bounty without detracting permanently from its value and, above all, maintain a living balance between man's actions and nature's reactions, for this nation's great resource is as elastic and productive as our ingenuity can make it.

> Remarks at the University of Wyoming, Laramie,
> September 25, 1963

Water is our most precious asset, and its potential uses are so many and so vital that they are frequently in conflict. Power versus irrigation; irrigation versus navigation; navigation versus industrial; industrial versus recreational.

> Remarks at the dedication of the Oahe Dam, Pierre, South Dakota,
> August 17, 1962

Specifically, we must extend our national energy resources base in order to promote our nation's economic growth.

> Letter to the Atomic Energy Commission on the development of
> civilian nuclear power, March 20, 1962

In the United States, some areas are desperately short of water—and at the same time other areas are ravaged by floods. And our forests are vanishing, our wildlife is vanishing, our streams are polluted and so is the very air we breathe.

Yet America is rich in natural resources. Our impending resource crisis is not due to scarcity. It is due to under-development, despoilment and neglect.

> Campaign remarks, Redding, California, September 8, 1960

In the long run, the public development of natural resources too vast for private capital—and federally encouraged research, especially basic research—are both sources of tremendous economic progress.

> Campaign remarks, New York, October 12, 1960

CHAPTER 9

Human Rights and Civil Liberties

John Kennedy's election as president accelerated the significant political movement toward more equal rights—nearly a century after the Civil War. Although the U.S. Supreme Court had used the 1954 *Brown v. Board of Education* case to reject as unconstitutional the concept of "separate but equal" in public education, frustrations remained great and tensions remained high over the slow pace of integration and equal access to jobs, housing, mass transit, and public services.

On the campaign trail, Kennedy spoke at conventions of black organizations, characterized civil rights as a "moral" issue, and criticized the Eisenhower administration's record on racial affairs. Kennedy won with strong support from African-American voters and leaders, but the new president also needed the support of conservative white Democrats in Congress to pursue his wider legislative priorities. Once in office, Kennedy found himself criticized by Rev. Martin Luther King Jr. and other activists as too moderate in enforcing federal civil rights protections. But even in balancing competing political realities, the president articulately expressed a commitment to an equal America and launched administrative and legislative initiatives toward that goal, including the broadest federal civil rights law ever introduced in Congress.

Meanwhile, Kennedy was ahead of most political contemporaries in advocating protection for women's rights. On the civil liberties front, his experience with the poisoned atmosphere of the McCarthy era sensitized him to the importance of safeguarding political freedoms. And, despite Kennedy's own run-ins with the press, he remained a staunch defender of First Amendment freedoms.

Civil Rights

Racial, religious, sex, and age discrimination must be eradicated to keep faith with our ideals and to strengthen our resources and speed our growth.

Manpower Report of the President, March 11, 1963

So I don't think we can undo the past. In fact, the past is going to be with us for a good many years in uneducated men and women who lost their chance for a decent education. We have to do the best we can now. That is what we are trying to do. I don't think quotas are a good idea. I think it is a mistake to assign quotas on the basis of religion, or race, or color, or nationality. I think we'd get into a good deal of trouble.

Our whole view of ourselves is a sort of one society. That has not been true. At least, that is where we are trying to go. I think that we ought not to begin the quota system. On the other hand, I do think that we ought to make an effort to give a fair chance to everyone who is qualified—not through a quota, but just look over our employment rolls, look over our areas where we are hiring people and at least make sure we are giving everyone a fair chance. But not hard and fast quotas. We are too mixed, this society of ours, to begin to divide ourselves on the basis of race or color.

Press conference, August 20, 1963

Whereas the Emancipation Proclamation and the 13th, 14th and 15th amendments to the Constitution of the United States guaranteed to Negro citizens equal rights with all other citizens of the United States and have made possible great progress toward the enjoyment of these rights; and

Whereas the goal of equal rights for all our citizens is still unreached, and the security of these rights is one of the great unfinished tasks of our democracy....

I call upon all citizens of the United States and all officials of the United States and of every state and local government to dedicate themselves to the completion of the task of assuring that every American, regardless of his race, religion, color or national origin, enjoys all the rights guaranteed by the Constitution and laws of the United States.

Emancipation Proclamation Centennial, December 28, 1962

There is no place for second-class citizenship in America.

Campaign statement, Hyannis, Massachusetts, August 6, 1960

I am also directing a complete study of current government employment practices—an examination of the status of members of minority groups in every department, agency and office of the federal government. When this survey—the most thorough ever undertaken—is completed we will have an accurate assessment of our present position and a yardstick by which to measure future progress.

I have dedicated my administration to the cause of equal opportunity in employment by the government and its contractors.

Statement on equal employment opportunity, March 6, 1961

We serve ourselves and the stature of freedom throughout the world by serving our moral commitment to equality.

Labor Day statement, August 29, 1961

This government will do whatever must be done to preserve order, to protect the lives of its citizens and to uphold the law of the land....

The federal government will not permit it to be sabotaged by a few extremists on either side who think they can defy both the law and the wishes of responsible citizens by inciting or inviting violence.

Remarks following the renewal of racial strife in Birmingham, Alabama, May 12, 1963

The Department of Defense has made great progress since the end of World War II in promoting equality of treatment and opportunity for all persons in the Armed Forces. The military services can take justifiable pride in their outstanding accomplishments in this area over the past ten years.

It is appropriate now, however, to make a thorough review of the current situation both within the services and in the communities where military installments are located to determine what further measures may be required to assure equality of treatment for all persons serving in the Armed Forces.

There is considerable evidence that in some civilian communities in which military installations are located, discrimination on the basis of race, color, creed or national origin is a serious source of hardship and embarrassment for Armed Forces personnel and their dependents....

What measures should be taken to improve the effectiveness of current policies and procedures in the Armed Forces with regard to equality of treatment and opportunity for persons in the Armed Forces?

What measures should be employed to improve equality of opportunity for members of the Armed Forces and their dependents in the civilian community, particularly with respect to housing, education, transportation, recreational facilities, community events, programs and activities?

> Letter to the Committee on Equal Opportunity in the
> Armed Forces, June 24, 1962

The right to vote is very basic. If we're going to neglect that right, then all of our talk about freedom is hollow. Therefore we shall give every protection that we can to anybody seeking to vote.

> Press conference, September 13, 1962

It is neither proper nor equitable that Americans should be denied the benefits of housing owned by the federal government or financed through federal assistance on the basis of their race, color, creed, or national origin.

Our national policy is equal opportunity for all, and the federal government will continue to take such legal and proper steps as it may to achieve the realization of this goal.

> Press conference, November 20, 1962

Indeed, discrimination in education is one basic cause of the other inequities and hardships inflicted upon our Negro citizens. The lack of equal educational opportunity deprives the individual of equal economic opportunity, restricts his contribution as a citizen and community leader, encourages him to drop out of school and imposes a heavy burden on the effort to eliminate discriminatory practices and prejudices from our national life.

> Message to Congress on civil rights and job opportunities,
> June 19, 1963

A peaceful revolution for human rights—demanding an end to racial discrimination in all parts of our community life—has strained at the leashes imposed by timid executive leadership.

> Democratic nomination acceptance speech, Los Angeles,
> July 15, 1960

This is no time for schools to close for any reason, and certainly no time for schools to be closed in the name of racial discrimination.

> Message for the Commission on Civil Rights conference on
> Schools in Transition, February 25, 1961

There are a good many millions of Americans who live in a family atmosphere which denies them equality of opportunity, not by law, although of course that is done too much in the United States, but by the very force of economic pressure upon them.

> Remarks to Delta Sigma Theta sorority, January 12, 1963

As chief executive, the next president must be prepared to put an end to racial and religious discrimination in every field of federal activity. He must issue executive orders which will do so. He must be willing to use the full resources of the executive agencies—from the Commission on Civil Rights to the Department of Health, Education and Welfare to explore every means of progress in this field, by conference, consultation and technical assistance.

Finally, as a moral leader, the next president must play an active creative role in interpreting the great human and moral issues involved. He cannot stand above the battle. He must exert the great moral and educational force of his office to create an affirmative new atmosphere in which further steps forward can be taken. The president, the representative of all interests and all sections, can promote the understanding and tolerance which is necessary if we are to complete the transition to a completely free society.

> Answer to a question from the *Washington Daily News*,
> published on October 11, 1960

I'm not satisfied until every American enjoys his full constitutional rights....I don't want the talents of any American to go to waste.

> Debate with Vice President Richard Nixon, Chicago,
> September 26, 1960

These are the questions and these areas that the North and South, East and West are entitled to know what will be the leadership of the president in these areas to provide equality of opportunity for employment, equality of opportunity in the field of housing, which could be done on all federal supported housing by a stroke of the president's pen.

What will be done to provide equality of education in all sections of the United States? Those are the questions to which the president must establish a moral tone and moral leadership....

Everyone who does business with the government should have the opportunity to make sure that they do not practice discrimination in their hiring, and that's in all sections of the United States.

And then [the president operates] as a moral leader. There is a very strong moral basis for this concept of equality before the law. Not only equality before the law, but also equality of opportunity. We are in a very difficult time. We need all the talent we can get. We sit on a conspicuous stage. We are a goldfish bowl before the world. We have to practice what we preach. We set a very high standard for ourselves....

We preach in the Declaration of Independence and in the Constitution, in the statements of our greatest leaders, we preach very high standards; and if we're not going to be charged before the world with hypocrisy, we have to meet those standards.

> Debate with Vice President Richard Nixon, October 7, 1960

The financial history of those communities which have been beset with racial disturbances shows that they attract less capital and less business.

> Address to the U.S. Conference of Mayors, Honolulu,
> June 9, 1963

The labor movement, after all, was originated by those who were being denied their equal opportunity. Whether it was because they were working six or seven days a week, whether it was because they were immigrants, whether it was because of one reason or another, the labor movement began as a union of those who were the least privileged in our society.

So it seems to me very natural that those who took into their ranks and, indeed, built their ranks upon the immigrants, upon women who were exploited, among men who worked too long, upon young people who were put to work under adverse conditions, old people who were dismissed when they were too old to sustain the burden of long employment, that the labor movement would be, as it has been for the last thirty years, the natural center and core of the effort to provide better opportunity for all of our fellow citizens.

Whatever their racial descent, whatever region of the country they come from. This is a cause to which labor has been associated with for fifty years.

> Remarks on signing a joint statement on fair employment
> practices, November 15, 1962

It is the duty of government to concern itself with protecting the opportunity to enjoy...basic liberties.

> Letter to the National Conference of Christians and Jews,
> October 10, 1960

"Our Constitution is color-blind," wrote Mr. Justice Harlan [of the U.S. Supreme Court] before the turn of the century, "and neither knows nor tolerates classes among citizens." But the practices of the country do not always conform to the principles of the Constitution....

Equality before the law has not always meant equal treatment and opportunity. And the harmful, wasteful and wrongful results of racial discrimination and segregation still appear in virtually every aspect of national life, in virtually every part of the nation....

The cruel disease of discrimination knows no sectional or state boundaries. The continuing attack on this problem must be equally broad.

Message to Congress on civil rights, February 28, 1963

It is regrettable that public disparagement of law and order has encouraged violence which has fallen on the innocent. If these cruel and tragic events can only awaken that city [Birmingham] and state [Alabama]—if they can only awaken this entire nation—to a realization of the folly of racial injustice and hatred and violence, then it is not too late for all concerned to unite in steps toward peaceful progress before more lives are lost.

Statement on the bombing in Birmingham, Alabama,
September 16, 1963

Civil Liberties

In 1776, Benjamin Franklin—fully aware of the risk—decided to entrust secret plans of the American Revolution to a French agent. He believed the man's word of honor that even British torture would never wring the facts from him. What more could he ask? "He would have given me his oath for it," Franklin reported to the Continental Congress, "if I laid stress upon oaths. But I have never regarded them otherwise than as the last recourse of liars."

Franklin knew that many an American agent had hypocritically taken the new British oath of allegiance. On the other hand, he knew that little could be expected from those colonists with Tory sympathies who had been compelled by their crusading neighbors to take oaths supporting the Revolution.

Unfortunately the American nation born in that year of divided loyalties has rarely heeded Ben Franklin's sage advice. In times of crisis to the state—times of war, insurrection or suspected subversion—both federal and state governments have repeatedly sought some swift, convenient and reassuring means of publicly identifying and compelling citizen loyalty. Elaborate loyalty oaths and affidavits—going far beyond the simple pledge of allegiance or the oath to uphold and defend the Constitution—have inevitably been the answer.

But there is no evidence that they have ever contributed substantially to the security of the nation.

Yet overzealous patriots keep trying to legislate loyalty.

Article in *Esquire* Magazine, April 1960

The historical background of this kind of special oath is not confined to the recent era of hate and suspicion. The first soldier in Washington's army to hang for treason—in a plot to capture the Continental Congress—had sworn to two special oaths of loyalty.

Article in *Coronet* Magazine, "Let's Get Rid of
College Loyalty Oaths!" April 1960

Disagreement and dissent are fundamental to a free society.

Address to the Committee for Economic Development,
May 9, 1963

I call upon the citizens of the United States to honor our heritage... and gain new strength for the long struggle against the forces of terror that threaten the freedoms which give meaning to human existence—the right to speak without fear and to seek the truth regardless of frontiers; the right to worship in accord with conscience and to share the strengths and glory of religion with our children; the right to determine our own institutions of government and to vote in secret for the candidate of our choice; the right to justice under law and to protection against arbitrary arrest; the right to labor and to join in efforts to improve conditions of work; the right to unite with our fellows, without distinction as to race, creed or color, in tearing down the walls of prejudice, ignorance and poverty wherever they may be, and to build ever firmer the foundations of liberty and equality for all.

Human Rights Week proclamation, December 9, 1961

Many a great nation has been torn by religious feuds and holy wars—but never the United States of America. For here diversity has led to unity—liberty has led to strength.

> Campaign remarks, Salt Lake City, September 23, 1960

Liberty calls for certain qualities of self-restraint and character which go with self-government.

> Campaign remarks, Los Angeles, September 9, 1960

The very word "secrecy" is repugnant in a free and open society, and we are as a people inherently and historically opposed to secret societies, to secret oaths and to secret proceedings. We decided long ago that the dangers of excessive and unwarranted concealment of pertinent facts far outweighed the dangers which are cited to justify it. Even today, there is little value in opposing the threat of a closed society by imitating its arbitrary restrictions. Even today, there is little value in insuring the survival of our nation if our traditions do not survive with it.

And there is very grave danger that an announced need for increased security will be seized upon by those anxious to expand its meaning to the very limits of official censorship and concealment. And no official of my administration, whether his rank is high or low, civilian or military, should interpret my words here tonight as an excuse to censor the news, to stifle dissent, to cover up our mistakes or to withhold from the press and the public the facts they deserve to know.

> Address to the American Newspaper Publishers Association,
> New York, April 27, 1961

Freedom [to disagree] is one of the penalties of democracy.

> *Why England Slept,* 1940

Women's Rights

One-third of our working force are women. They have a primary obligation to their families and their homes, but…their work makes it possible to maintain that home and that family in many cases. We want to make sure that they are able to move ahead and perform their functions without any discrimination by law or by implication.

> Remarks to the President's Commission on the Status of Women, February 12, 1962

We are attempting to make sure that the women, for example, who work—one-third of our working force are women—we want to try to encourage every company in the United States and certainly stimulate governmental leadership on providing equal pay and equal conditions for women.

> Interview with Eleanor Roosevelt for National Educational Television, April 22, 1962

Undoubtedly the ever-advancing frontier in our country helped to break down attitudes carried over from feudal days. But we have by no means done enough to strengthen family life and at the same time encourage women to make their full contribution as citizens.

> Statement on the President's Commission on the Status of Women, December 14, 1961

This used to be an old story, that a civilization could be judged on how it treated its elderly people. But I think it can also be judged on its opportunities for women.

> Remarks on the final report of the President's Commission on the Status of Women, October 11, 1963

I sometimes wonder whether we make as much use of all of our talent that we have in this country as we should. I think particularly of the hundreds of thousands and millions of women teachers, doctors, flyers, a whole variety of skills which they possess which I think we should use to the maximum. And I am concerned that we sometimes do not for one reason or another.

> Remarks to the "99 Club" of Women Pilots, July 24, 1963

I intend that the federal career service be maintained in every respect without discrimination and with equal opportunity for employment and advancement.

> Memorandum on equal opportunity for women in the federal service, July 24, 1962

It will be forty-two years tomorrow since women gained the right to participate fully in the governing of our country through the right to vote. It is appropriate on this date, therefore, that we take note of the progress made and the distance to be traveled to achieve full equality for all of our citizens.

> Letter to Eleanor Roosevelt, August 26, 1962

I must say I am a strong believer in equal pay for equal work, and I think we ought to do better than we're doing.

> Press conference, November 9, 1961

International Human Rights

No government or social system is so evil that its people must be considered as lacking in virtue. As Americans, we find communism profoundly repugnant as a negation of personal freedom and dignity. But we can still hail the Russian people for their many achievements—in science and space, in economic and industrial growth, in culture and in acts of courage.

> Commencement address at American University, June 10, 1963

The cause of human rights and dignity, some two centuries after its birth, in Europe and the United States, is still moving men and nations with ever-increasing momentum.

> Address at the Free University, Berlin, Germany, June 26, 1963

The American people will be assured that this government's leadership will be maintained in the great humanitarian endeavor of helping the world's stateless and homeless people. In continuing this endeavor, we will be carrying forward a great American tradition which is as well-known as the generosity of our people in coming to the aid of those in need.

> Statement on the Migration and Refugee Assistance Act,
> June 28, 1962

Great strides have been made in alleviating many of the world's refugee and migration problems.... Yet millions of refugees are still in desperate want in many parts of the world and the foreboding atmosphere of political conditions and the oppression of communism gives continuing warning of more refugees to come.

The United States must be prepared at all times to act promptly and effectively to help these new refugee groups as they emerge and to show our humanitarian concern for those who seek freedom as the unwilling and unfortunate victims of war and violence.

> Letter to Congress on refugee aid legislation, July 21, 1961

CHAPTER 10

The American Economy

The United States had been buffeted by recessions and slow economic recovery in the years before John Kennedy assumed power—and recession meant high unemployment, budget deficits, a trade deficit, and shortage of badly needed development. While campaigning for president, Kennedy decried the sluggish growth of the Eisenhower years. But he gained little immediate success in this domain after assuming the presidency, and the economy remained his most serious domestic challenge.

Because strong labor support had elected Kennedy, he recognized a need to court business leaders for support—but privately chastised oil companies and other industries that he regarded as obstructing his economic initiatives. Believing his Treasury secretary would be one of his two most important Cabinet choices, he found a moderate Republican with a banking background to take the job. At the same time, he chose liberal economic advisers, telling one of them, "You'll find that I'm a good deal more interested in economics than my predecessor, and maybe a little bit better informed on it."

As in so many other areas, Kennedy saw complex connections between economic performance and America's international strength and influence. He wrestled with stock market fluctuations and with strikes and threatened strikes involving shipping, the automobile industry, newspapers, railroads, and construction. There were policy decisions to make about price and wage controls, about trade tariffs and about tax cuts. The administration's efforts helped raise American industrial productivity, worker salaries, and consumer spending, but unemployment persisted at a troublingly high rate.

Government's Role in the Economy

I receive no mail thanking me and expressing admiration for my economic wisdom when the market goes up, but when it goes down we all know who is wrong.

Address to the Advertising Council, March 13, 1963

There is no long-range hostility between business and the government. There cannot be. We cannot succeed unless they succeed. But that doesn't mean that we should not meet our responsibilities under antitrust, or that doesn't mean when we attempt to pass a bill on taxes to prevent tax havens abroad or a flood of capital which affects our gold balances—that doesn't mean we're anti-business. It means that we have to meet our public responsibilities. In the long run, most businessmen know that we are allied—as we are with labor and the farmer—in trying to keep this country going.

Press conference, November 8, 1961

No nation in the history of the world has ever experienced a century of economic growth comparable to that of the United States in the last 100 years. In 100 years, the growth of our free enterprise economy under a free political system, and under the development effectively of our national and local and state educational systems, has brought our citizens to an unprecedented standard of living. It has brought to our nation an unparalleled position in the world, as the world's foremost banker, merchant, manufacturer and consumer....

All this has been made possible by economic growth.

And yet we have heard in recent times that economic growth is too abstract a concept; that it is too academic for politicians and voters; that it is too theoretical a basis for proposals to the Congress. I do not see anything abstract or academic about economic growth.

> Remarks at the American Bankers Association's Symposium on
> Economic Growth, February 25, 1963

The federal income tax is one of those subjects about which we talk, about which we complain, but about which not very much is done. Perhaps we have heard too long about the certainty of "death and taxes."

> Address on the Test Ban Treaty and Tax Reduction Bill,
> September 18, 1963

It is increasingly clear that nations united in freedom are better able to build their economies than those that are repressed by tyranny.

> Remarks at NATO headquarters, Naples, Italy, July 2, 1963

We must extend our national energy resources base in order to promote our nation's economic growth.

> Letter to the Atomic Energy Commission on the development of
> civilian nuclear power, March 20, 1962

As president my interest is in an economy which will be strong enough to absorb the potential of a rapidly expanding population, steady enough to avert the wide swings which bring grief to so many of our people and non-inflationary enough to persuade investors that this country holds a steady promise of growth and stability.

My specific interest at this time is in maintaining a competitive world position that will not further stir the gold in Fort Knox.

> Address to the U.S. Chamber of Commerce, April 30, 1962

This country cannot prosper unless business prospers. This country cannot meet its obligations—its tax obligations and all the rest—unless business is doing well. Business will not do well and you will not have full employment unless they feel that there's a chance to make profit.

> Press conference, November 8, 1961

Tax reform, of course, is a wonderful principle. But when you begin to write it in detail, it becomes less attractive.

Press conference, February 14, 1963

I know that when things don't go well, businessmen like to blame the presidents, and that's one of the things which presidents are paid for.

Press conference, June 14, 1962

A prosperous and growing economy is a major objective in its own right. It is also the primary means by which to achieve a balance in our federal budget and in our balance of payments.

Press conference, July 17, 1963

Private investment goes where there is a return on capital, which may or may not serve the particular national need of the time. Sometimes it does. On occasions it may not be so useful.

Remarks to student leaders from Brazil, July 30, 1963

Credit unions have had a long history of service. They perform a valuable function—permitting people to pool their resources and attain greater economic security. It is a form of self-help in the best American tradition.

Statement on Credit Union Day, October 17, 1963

The nation's challenge to meet the needs of defense mobilization and to achieve national and international economic stability and development cannot be fully met if any part of the country is unproductive and unstable economically.

"Economic Problems of New England: A Program for Congressional Action," 1953

All of us in government and in business should be thinking of what additional steps we could take which would be of assistance in maintaining an economic growth rate which will absorb the increase in our population and also those who are technologically dislocated.

Press conference, September 26, 1962

Economic progress at home is still the first requirement for economic strength abroad.

> Message to Congress on gold and the balance of payments deficit, February 6, 1961

It is well to remind ourselves from time to time of the benefits we derive from the maintenance of a free market system. The system rests on freedom of consumer choice, the profit motive, and vigorous competition for the buyer's dollar. By relying on these spontaneous economic forces, we secure these benefits:

Our system tends automatically to produce the kinds of goods that consumers want in the relative quantities in which people want them.

The system tends automatically to minimize waste. If one producer is making a product inefficiently, another will see an opportunity for profit by making the product at a lower cost.

The system encourages innovation and technological change. High profits are the reward of the innovator, but competitors will soon adopt the new techniques, thus forcing the innovator to continue to push ahead.

> Press conference, September 26, 1962

Once given a fair and equal opportunity to compete in overseas markets, and once subject to healthy competition from overseas manufacturers for our own markets, American management and labor will have additional reason to maintain competitive costs and prices, modernize their plants and increase their productivity. The discipline of the world market place is an excellent measure of efficiency and a force to stability.

> Message to Congress on foreign trade policy, January 25, 1962

To keep pace with the growth of our economy and national defense requirements, expansion of this nation's power facilities will require intensive effort by all segments of our power industry.... Sustained heavy expansion by all power suppliers—public, cooperative and private—is clearly needed.

The role of the federal government in supplying an important segment of this power is now long established and must continue. We will meet our responsibilities in this field.

> Message to Congress on natural resources, February 23, 1961

But your statement of principles can only be a beginning. In the last analysis, high ethical standards can be achieved only through voluntary effort....

I am confident that American business will respond, but in addition to helping businessmen, your work should assist the general public to achieve a broader understanding of these problems—for ethics is a matter of concern for us all.

> Statement to Business Ethics Advisory Council, January 16, 1962

The popular fear of deficits arises from the fact that what is sound policy at one time can be unsound policy at another. When there are more empty jobs than people seeking them, when industrial capacity is fully utilized, then it would be not only unsound but dangerous for the federal government to raise its expenditures without raising taxes, or to cut taxes without an equal cut in expenditures.

The American people have learned that lesson, as have the governments of other nations, and some of them are learning it the hard way today.

> Address to the Committee for Economic Development, May 9, 1963

Confronting Crisis and Challenges

This administration has not undertaken and will not undertake to fix prices and wages in this economy. We have no intention of intervening in every labor dispute. We are neither able nor willing to substitute our judgment for the judgment of those who sit at the local bargaining tables across the country. We can suggest guidelines for the economy but we cannot fix a single pattern for every plant and every industry.

> Address to the United Auto Workers, Atlantic City, New Jersey, May 8, 1962

I am establishing a board of inquiry to inquire into the labor dispute in the maritime industry.

There have already been serious interruptions in the movement of food, oil and other essential commodities. The supply lifelines to the state of Hawaii and to Puerto Rico have been cut. There have been delays in the shipments of military cargoes.

Statement on the maritime strike, June 26, 1961

This nation continues to be troubled about its balance-of-payment deficit, which, despite its decline, remains a stubborn and troublesome problem.

State of the Union Address, January 14, 1963

As we in America seek to complete our own Revolution by dignifying human life with the material securities we produce and the spiritual freedoms we protect, the mass of the world's people embark on their own economic and social awakening from the long slumber of the past.

Letter to AFL-CIO president George Meany, June 28, 1961

Although we do not today face a problem of general recession, the two recessions of the last five years—interrupted only by a short and incomplete recovery—have left in their wake serious problems of prolonged large-scale unemployment and economic distress in hundreds of communities in all sections of the country. The roster of these communities includes large cities, smaller cities and rural areas.

The causes of their troubles are manifold—exodus of industry, displacement of labor by technological change, excessive dependence on declining industries, influx of job-seekers, changing weapons requirements in military procurement, and chronic rural poverty.

Letter to Congress proposing a capital works program, March 26, 1962

The national interest can be protected and the interests of the industry and the employees forwarded through free and responsible collective bargaining.

Telephone message to industry and union leaders after the steel industry settlement, March 31, 1962

Simultaneous and identical actions of United States Steel and other leading steel corporations increasing steel prices by some $6 a ton constitute a wholly unjustifiable and irresponsible defiance of the public interest....

The American people will find it hard, as I do, to accept a situation in which a tiny handful of steel executives whose pursuit of private power and profit exceeds their sense of public responsibility can show such utter contempt for the interests of 185 million Americans.

Price and wage decisions, except for a very limited restriction in the case of monopolies and national emergency strikes, are and ought to be freely and privately made. But the American people have a right to expect, in return for that freedom, a higher sense of business responsibility for the welfare of their country than has been shown in the last two days.

Press conference, April 11, 1962

This administration is not interested in determining the appropriate price or profit level of any particular industry. We are interested in protecting the American public.

Statement on the need for price and wage stability in the
steel industry, April 11, 1963

Creating Jobs and Economic Opportunities

It is a fact that we have to find, over a ten-year period, 25,000 new jobs every week to take care of those who are displaced by machines and those who are coming into the labor market, so that this places a major burden upon our economy and on our society, and it's one to which we will have to give our attention in the next decade....I regard it as the major domestic challenge, really, of the sixties, to maintain full employment at a time when automation, of course, is replacing men.

Press conference, February 14, 1962

Working together, business and government must do better—putting people back to work, using plants to capacity and spurring savings and investments with at least a large part of our economic gains—beginning not when our economy is back at the top but beginning now.

> Address to the National Industrial Conference Board,
> February 13, 1961

I know that statistics and details of the economy may sometimes seem dry, but the economy and economic statistics are really a story of all of us as a country, and these statistics tell whether we are going forward or standing still or going backward. They tell whether an unemployed man can get a job or whether a man who has a job can get an increase in salary or own a home or whether he can retire in security or send his children to college. These are the people and the things behind the statistics.

> Report to the American People on the state of the
> national economy, August 13, 1962

We did not think that defense bases should be kept going... when there was no longer a need for them in order to maintain the defensive strength of the United States. I think that is a traditional position and one which this administration will follow. We will attempt to the best of our ability to maintain jobs for the people who are involved, but we cannot get a strong national defense if we continue defense systems or bases which are archaic and outmoded, and which no long represent a real need. I am hopeful that the country's economy generally will be strong enough to absorb those who may be thrown out of work because of structural changes in our defense system. But I think it is a serious problem, as we change from planes to missiles, you affect employment not only in the bases but in the defense industries themselves.

> Press conference, April 12, 1961

CHAPTER 11

The News Media

Even before entering politics, John Kennedy was no stranger to the ways of the press. When he left the Navy after recovering from war injuries, he worked as a newspaper reporter covering the United Nations Conference in San Francisco, and his future wife, Jacqueline Bouvier, spent a stint as a newspaper photographer. He became the nation's first truly "television president," as the 1960 campaign was more fully televised than any previous election and many observers credit his performance during televised debates as the decisive factor in his narrow victory over Vice President Richard Nixon. In 1961 alone, Kennedy held nineteen televised press conferences. Biographer Richard Reeves described how Kennedy's dominance of that forum "changed the journalism of Washington, and, to a large extent, that changed the presidency and government itself."

Even so, Kennedy was troubled by what he regarded as press reports helpful to the "enemy"—the communists. In one speech, he urged the press to exercise "self-discipline"—meaning self-censorship—and to help his administration design guidelines for Cold War coverage. Kennedy also realized that the press was far more critical of who he was and how he ran the government than it had been when he was merely one of one hundred senators, or even the presidential nominee. Kennedy's irritation with the press was often readily apparent—for example, his complaint about "the tendency both in Washington and Saigon to fight our battles via the newspapers."

Media Influence

The American press has substantial influence around the world. We do not read—foreign leaders do not read—the American press necessarily as we read the Soviet press to find out what the official governmental policy is. [Yet] quite obviously there is an intimate relationship between your work, your responsibility, and the work that we are doing and our responsibility.

Press conference, June 8, 1961

Any newspaper strike is unfortunate because it affects the whole community, the distribution of news and business.

Press conference, May 9, 1962

It is true, however, that when a well-known diplomat from another country demanded recently that our State Department repudiate certain newspaper attacks on his colleague it was unnecessary for us to reply that this administration was not responsible for the press, for the press had already made it clear that it was not responsible for this administration.

Address to the American Newspaper Publishers Association,
New York, April 27, 1961

I sometimes think we are too much impressed by the clamor of daily events. The newspaper headlines and the television screens give us a short view. They so flood us with the stop-press detail of daily stories that we lose sight of…the great movements of history. Yet it is the profound tendencies of history, and not the passing excitements, that will shape our future.

Address at the University of California at Berkeley,
March 23, 1962

In 1851, the *New York Herald Tribune*, under the sponsorship of Horace Greeley, included as its London correspondent an obscure journalist by the name of Karl Marx. We are told that the foreign correspondent, Marx, stone broke and with a family ill and undernourished, constantly appealed to Greeley and managing editor Charles Dana for an increase in his munificent salary of $5 per installment, a salary which he and [communism theoretician Friedrich] Engels labeled as the "lousiest petty bourgeois cheating."

But when all his financial appeals were refused, Marx looked around for other means of livelihood and fame, and eventually terminated his relationship with the *Tribune* and devoted his talents full time to the cause that would bequeath to the world the seeds of Leninism, Stalinism, revolution and the Cold War.

If only this capitalist New York newspaper had treated him more kindly, if only Marx had remained a foreign correspondent, history might have been different, and I hope all publishers will bear this lesson in mind the next time they receive a poverty-stricken appeal for a small increase in the expense account from an obscure newspaperman.

> Address to the American Newspaper Publishers Association, New York, April 27, 1961

Media Responsibility

You bastards [journalists] are getting more information out of the White House—the kind of information you want when you want it—than ever before. Except for the Cuba thing, I challenge you to give me an example of our managing the news.

> Conversation with Benjamin Bradlee of *Newsweek*, March 26, 1963

I do wish that some of the speeches I give would get as much attention as the speeches which I do not give.

> Presss conference, May 5, 1961

It is never pleasant to be reading things that are not agreeable news, but I would say it is an invaluable arm of the presidency, as a check really on what is going on in the administration, and more things come to my attention that cause me concern or give me information....

Now, on the other hand, the press has the responsibility not to distort things for political purposes, not to just take some news in order to prove a political point. It seems to me their obligation is to be as tough as they can on the administration but do it in a way which is directed toward getting as close to the truth as they can get and not merely because of some political motive.

> Broadcast interview, "After Two Years—a Conversation with
> the President," December 17, 1962

The American press prints a lot of bad news, because bad news is news and good news is not news.

> Ibid.

I think that they are doing their task, as a critical branch, the fourth estate. And I am attempting to do mine. And we are going to live together for a period, and then go our separate ways.

> Press conference, May 9, 1962

We have to make a judgment as to how much we can usefully say [to the press] that would aid the interest of the United States. One of the problems of a free society—a problem not met by a dictatorship—is this problem of information.

> Press conference, April 21, 1961

I have asked the newspaper industry, without much success, to exercise more self-restraint in publishing intelligence data helpful to any enemy.

> Letter to Alicia Patterson, editor and publisher of *Newsday*,
> May 16, 1961

For the facts of the matter are that this nation's foes have openly boasted of acquiring through our newspapers information they would otherwise hire agents to acquire through theft, bribery or espionage; that details of this nation's covert operations have been available to every newspaper reader, friend and foe alike; and that the size, the strength, the location and the nature of our forces and weapons, and our plans and strategy for their use, have all been pinpointed in the press and other news media to a degree sufficient to satisfy any foreign power; and that, in at least one case, the publication of details concerning a secret mechanism whereby satellites were followed required its alteration at the expense of considerable time and money.

These newspapers which printed these stories were loyal, patriotic, responsible and well-meaning. Had we been engaged in open warfare, they undoubtedly would not have published such items. But in the absence of open warfare, they recognized only the tests of journalism, and not the tests of national security.

> Address to the American Newspaper Publishers Association, New York, April 27, 1961

Can you find out where the newspaper stories came [from] this weekend on the Vietnam military intervention into southern Laos? Those stories were harmful to us. Probably exaggerated.

> Memo to Special Assistant for National Security Affairs McGeorge Bundy, August 14, 1961

We've had very limited success in managing the news, if that's what we have been trying to do.

> Press conference, February 21, 1963

CHAPTER 12

Culture and the Arts

Camelot, the popular musical that celebrated the legendary court of King Arthur, opened on Broadway scant weeks after John Kennedy was elected president. Though this timing was almost certainly coincidental, the two events became so indelibly linked in public consciousness that Camelot became a virtual synonym for the Kennedy White House and its unique cultural glamour—a mystique that endures through today.

To be sure, some of this allure can be attributed merely to the contrast with the plain Midwesternism of the White House's immediately previous occupants: Harry Truman of Missouri and Dwight D. Eisenhower of Kansas. No matter how fiercely partisan the attacks against them, nobody could possibly have accused either of those presidents or their wives (plainspoken Bessie and Mamie, respectively) of being would-be cultural sophisticates.

Yet the glamorous aura of the Kennedy White House was much more than a matter of contrast. For example, nearly 160 scholars, artists, and creative leaders were invited to the inauguration. As August Heckscher, Kennedy's first White House cultural coordinator, later reminisced, "I don't think he had any idea of the reverberations or the expectations that it would create in the mind of the artistic community. They all said, 'Now that the President has done this, what is he going to do next?'"

Indeed, in Kennedy's slightly more than one thousand days in office, his White House elevated the arts and high culture to a remarkable prominence. But unquestionably, the key figure in this regard was Jacqueline Lee Bouvier Kennedy. Educated at the best private schools, she studied ballet, traveled extensively, and spent her junior year abroad in France before graduating from George Washington University.

It is not surprising that within a month of becoming First Lady, she set up the White House Fine Arts Committee with experts in historic preservation and decorative arts and personally supervised the White House restoration. After establishing the White House Historical Association, she conducted a memorable televised tour of the White House in February 1962, seen by an estimated 56 million viewers. Under her influence—and the president's encouragement—the White House became a deliberate showcase for America's leading performance arts organizations to an unprecedented extent. As Jacqueline Kennedy commented, her goal "was to present the best in the arts, not necessarily what was popular at the time."

I have never taken the view that the world of politics and the world of poetry are so far apart. I think politicians and poets share at least one thing, and that is that their greatness depends upon the courage with which they face the challenges of life.

> Remarks on the television program "Robert Frost: American Poet," February 26, 1961

I have long believed, as you know, that the quality of America's cultural life is an element of immense importance in the scales by which our worth will ultimately be weighed.

> Letter to August Heckscher, June 17, 1963

We are a very self-critical society.... We read more books than any other country.... We have more people going to traveling arts shows than any other country in the world.

We are, even though we hesitate to admit it, a cultured people and I hope we will be more so.

> Remarks at White House musical program for youth, April 22, 1963

Establishment of an Advisory Council on the Arts has long seemed a natural step in fulfilling the government's responsibility to the arts....The creation of this council means that for the first time the arts will have some formal government body which will be specifically concerned with all aspects of the arts and to which the artist and the arts institutions can present their views and bring their problems.

> Statement on establishing the Advisory Council on the Arts,
> June 12, 1963

As an American, I have the greatest possible pride in the work that's being done in dozens of schools stretching across the United States—schools where devoted teachers are studying with interested young men and women and opening up the whole wide horizon of serious music.

> Remarks at White House concert for handicapped children,
> August 22, 1961

The United States, one of the newest of civilizations, has long had a deep regard for the study of past cultures, and a concern for the preservation of man's great achievements of art and thought.

We have also had a special interest in the civilization of ancient Egypt from which many of our own cultural traditions have sprung—and a deep friendship for the people who live in the valley of the Nile.

> Letter to Congress concerning preservation of ancient
> monuments in the Nile Valley, April 7, 1961

It is no accident that men of genius in music like [Ignacy Jan] Paderewski or [Frederic] Chopin should also have been great patriots. You have to be a free man to be a great artist.

> Remarks on dedication of marker to identify Paderewski's grave,
> Arlington, Virginia, May 9, 1963

Every major capital in the world, and a good many capitals of states which are not large, has a center which demonstrates the performing arts, serves as the place for exhibiting the finest in the nation's cultural life. Washington does not have one and I think this country suffers.

> Remarks on the National Cultural Center Act, August 19, 1963

We do not manage our cultural life in this country, nor does any free society, but it is an important part. It is one of the great purposes....

There are so many more people playing a musical instrument now, going to symphonies, going to the theater, to art galleries, painting, than anyone realizes. And it is our hope that Americans will begin to look about them and realize that here in these years we are building a life which, as I say, develops the maximum in each individual.

> Toast to André Malraux, French Minister for Cultural Affairs,
> May 11, 1962

Someone sent me a letter last week, which was a copy of a letter which Thomas Jefferson wrote to a friend in Rome. He asked him to see if he could get three Italians to come over to help on his garden, and at the end of his letter he said, "Make sure that they all can play the violin and sing for my orchestra here at Monticello."

> Remarks at birthday salute to the President, New York,
> May 19, 1962

One of our great assets in this country are the talented boys and girls who devote their early lives to music, to appreciation of music, to an understanding of it. This is a great and I think vital force in American life. It is a part of American life which I think is somewhat unheralded around the world.

But this emphasis upon artistic achievement in music, I think, is a source of satisfaction and pride to all of us.

> Remarks at White House program for youth, April 16, 1962

Too often in the past, we have thought of the artist as an idler and dilettante and of the lover of arts as somehow sissy or effete. We have done both an injustice.

The life of the artist is, in relation to his work, stern and lonely. He has labored hard, often amid deprivation, to perfect his skill. He has turned aside from quick success in order to strip his vision of everything secondary or cheapening. His working life is marked by intense application and intense discipline.

As for the lover of the arts, it is he who, by subjecting himself to the sometimes disturbing experience of art, sustains the artist—and seeks only the reward that his life will, in consequence, be the more fully lived.

> Article in *Look* magazine, "The Arts in America,"
> December 18, 1962

Genius can speak at any time, and the entire world will hear it and listen. Behind the storm of daily conflict and crisis, the dramatic confrontations, the tumult of political struggle, the poet, the artist, the musician continues the quiet work of centuries, building bridges of experience between peoples, reminding man of the universality of his feelings and desires and despairs, and reminding him that the forces that unite are deeper than those that divide.

Thus, art and the encouragement of art is political in the most profound sense, not as a weapon in the struggle but as an instrument of understanding of the futility of struggle between those who share man's faith.

> Remarks on behalf of the National Culture Center,
> November 29, 1962

Books and libraries and the will to use them are among the most important tools our nation has to diffuse knowledge and to develop our powers of creative wisdom. It is, however, a fact that there is an important gap in the availability of books and libraries to our citizens.... There is a great imbalance of resources among the great educational institutions of our country....

The community public library is one of the richest and more enduring aspects of our historical heritage.

> Statement on National Library Week, April 16, 1961

In free society art is not a weapon and it does not belong to the sphere of polemics and ideology. Artists are not engineers of the soul. It may be different elsewhere. But democratic society—in it, the highest duty of the writer, the composer, the artist is to remain true to himself and to let the chips fall where they may.

> Remarks at Amherst College,
> Amherst, Massachusetts, October 26, 1963

We recognize increasingly the essentiality of artistic achievement. This is part, I think, of a nationwide movement toward excellence—a movement which had its start in the admiration of expertness and skill in our technical society, but which now demands quality in all realms of human achievement.

It is part, too, of a feeling that art is the great unifying and humanizing experience.... the side of life which expresses the emotions and embodies values and ideals of beauty.

"The Arts in America" in the book *Creative America*, 1962

I know that there is some feeling by Americans that the arts are developed in solitude, that they are developed by inspiration and by sudden fits of genius. But the fact of the matter is that success comes in music or in the arts like success comes in every other form of human endeavor—by hard work, by discipline, over a long period of time.

Remarks to the National High School Symphony Orchestra, August 6, 1962

I am certain that after the dust of centuries has passed over our cities, we, too, will be remembered not for victories or defeats in battle or in politics, but for our contribution to the human spirit.

Remarks on behalf of the National Cultural Center, November 29, 1962

When power leads man toward arrogance, poetry reminds him of his limitations. When power narrows the areas of man's concern, poetry reminds him of the richness and diversity of his existence. When power corrupts, poetry cleanses.

Remarks at Amherst College, Amherst, Massachusetts, October 26, 1963

CHAPTER 13

Parties and Partisan Politics

Politics seemed to run in John Kennedy's blood. He was grandson of Boston mayor John "Honey Fitz" Fitzgerald and son of Ambassador Joseph P. Kennedy. Not surprisingly, Democratic Party politics and elections were part of his upbringing and family life. Yet in a memoir he was dictating shortly before his 1960 victory, Kennedy acknowledged that he had held no political ambitions for himself until his older brother Joseph Jr. died in combat during World War II.

But once Kennedy took the plunge, he proved to be a potent politician—a self-described "total politician." In 1946, he won a Massachusetts congressional seat, and six years later, won a Senate election despite the landslide election of Republican president Dwight D. Eisenhower. In 1956, Kennedy was still in his first Senate term when he maneuvered unsuccessfully for his party's vice presidential nomination and then set his eyes on the White House itself.

The 1960 primary season was grueling as he competed for his party's presidential nomination. On the campaign trail—in stump speeches and rallies—Kennedy's charisma, vision, and youth provided vital strategic weapons against far more experienced rivals such as Senators Lyndon B. Johnson and

Hubert Humphrey. Then the general election gave him a narrow—and some Republicans say ethically tainted—victory over another military veteran, Vice President Richard Nixon.

Kennedy's political involvement certainly didn't end with his inauguration. Instead, he kept close control of his party and actively campaigned around the country on behalf of Democratic candidates for Congress and governorships. It's vital, however, to understand that Kennedy saw politics not merely as a game of power and ego, but as a noble calling: an emotionally and intellectually satisfying opportunity for public service.

Parties, Elections and Partisanship

I am all for debates because I believe—and I am going to debate when I am a candidate, if I am a candidate again—because I believe that this is the way the people of this state or other states or this country can make a judgment as to the competence and knowledge of those who present themselves for office....I believe they should all step forward and answer each other.

Remarks at a political rally, Trenton, New Jersey,
November 2, 1961

Election of the president of the United States is the supreme test of the democratic process in this country. Because the duly nominated candidates of both our national parties must campaign throughout the country, carrying their views to all the nation's voters, there are great financial burdens in conducting presidential campaigns.

To have presidential candidates dependent on large financial contributions of those with special interests is highly undesirable, especially in these days when the public interest requires basic decisions so essential to our national security and survival. The financial base of our presidential campaigns must be broadened.

Statement on the President's Commission on Campaign Costs,
October 4, 1961

I would never suggest that the battle of the mimeograph machines between the Republican and the Democratic Committees should cease, only that it should perhaps be wiser.

> Press conference, October 11, 1961

Quite honestly, no Democratic administration has banked heavily on the amount of support it would get politically from the business community.

> Press conference, September 26, 1962

I think we serve this country, and our party serves this country, when we tell the truth, when we present the facts, honestly and clearly, and give the American people an opportunity to make their judgment.

> Campaign remarks, Paducah, Kentucky, October 8, 1960

My judgment is that the Republican Party has stood still here in the United States, and it's also stood still around the world.

> Debate with Vice President Richard Nixon, New York,
> October 21, 1960

Political leaders come and go.

> Remarks at City Hall, Frankfurt, Germany, June 25, 1963

There is an old saying that a farmer votes Republican only if he can afford it. I don't think the farmer can afford to vote Republican in 1960. I think the farmer is in the position of the famous Mark Twain hero who rose rapidly from affluence to poverty.

> Campaign remarks, Wichita, Kansas, October 22, 1960

I am not sure that I am the most popular political figure in our country today in the South, but that is all right.

> Press conference, September 2, 1963

Be prepared to travel day and night, east and west, in an overheated limousine in 93-degree weather in Fort Lauderdale, Florida, and in raw 30-degree temperature in Bellows Falls, Vermont, and in Twin Falls, Idaho.

> Remarks in Boston, November 8, 1956

If we can lower the voting age to 9, we are going to sweep the state.

Campaign remarks, Girard, Ohio, October 9, 1960

I think one of the great myths in American life is that those who are in politics love to campaign. Well, maybe some do, but it's hard work making a lot of speeches, and I have a good many other things to do.

Interview with William Lawrence of ABC for
the television program "Politics '62," October 14, 1962

We should not be too hasty in condemning all compromise as bad morals. For politics and legislation are not matters for inflexible principles or unattainable ideals.

Profiles in Courage, 1956

Well, let me say I do think that parties are important in that they tell something about the program and something about the man.

Abraham Lincoln was a great president of all the people; but he was selected by his party at a key time in history because his party stood for something.

The Democratic party in this century has stood for something. It has stood for progress. It has stood for concern for the people's welfare. It has stood for a strong foreign policy and a strong national defense, and as a result produced [Woodrow] Wilson, President [Franklin] Roosevelt, and President [Harry] Truman. The Republican party has produced [William] McKinley, and [Warren] Harding, [Calvin] Coolidge, [Thomas] Dewey and [Alf] Landon. They do stand for something. They stand for a whole different approach to the problems facing this country at home and abroad.

Debate with Vice President Richard Nixon, October 7, 1960

It seems inconceivable to me that people can make speeches against unemployment and then vote to destroy a program the objective of which is to attack the unemployment problem by providing jobs, especially in those areas with chronic and persistent unemployment.

Statement concerning the Accelerated Public Works program,
April 6, 1963

I've learned that you don't get far in politics until you become a total politician. That means you've got to deal with the party leaders as well as the voters. From now on, I'm going to be a total politician.

Comment to advisors Kenneth O'Donnell and David Powers, 1956

I never thought at school or college that I would ever run for office myself. One politician was enough in the family, and my [older] brother Joe was obviously going to be that politician. I hadn't considered myself a political type, and he filled all the requirements for political success....

I didn't plan to get into it, and when I started out as a congressman, there were lots of things I didn't know, a lot of mistakes I made, maybe some votes that should have been different.

Interview with journalist Ed Plaut, 1960

My brother Joe was killed in Europe as a flier in August 1944 and that ended our hopes for him. But I didn't even start to think about a political profession for more than a year later.

Tape-recorded memoir entry, October 1960

Remember [Franklin D.] Roosevelt's principle that you have to keep politicians and policies apart.

Diary entry, January 23, 1946

Whatever other qualifications I may have had when I became president, one of them at least was that I knew Wisconsin better than any other president of the United States. That is an unchallengeable statement. My foot-tracks are in every house in this state.

Address at the Jefferson-Jackson Dinner, Milwaukee, May 12, 1962

I remember when I announced my candidacy [for Congress], I was slapped on the back by a great many lawyers, bankers and stockbrokers who wished me well and said they were glad to see young fellows going into politics. But that was the last I ever saw of them.

They helped neither me nor my opponents.

Speech at Choate School, Wallingford, Connecticut, September 27, 1946

Woodrow Wilson once said, "What use is a political party unless it is being served and being used by the nation for some great purpose?"

So the question, really, which both political parties must constantly face: what purpose do we serve, what good are we doing the nation, of all the problems that face us at home and abroad, how is our party, whether we are Democrats or Republicans, how are we measuring up, what is our program, what are the needs of the country and what are we doing about them?

> Remarks to Democratic State Committeewomen of California, Hollywood, June 8, 1963

Politics in American Life

Few other professions are so demanding, but few, I must add, are so satisfying to the heart and soul.

> *Harvard Alumni Bulletin,* May 19, 1956

The price of politics is high, but think of all those people living normal average lives who never touch the excitement of it.

> Interview with journalist Ed Plaut, 1960

It is disheartening to me, and I think alarming for our Republic, to realize how poorly the political profession is regarded in America. Mothers may still want their favorite sons to grow up to be president but, according to a famous Gallup poll of some years ago, they do not want them to become politicians in the process.

Unfortunately, this disdain for the political process is not only shared but intensified by the educational profession.

> Address to the American Association of School Administrators and National School Boards Association, February 21, 1957

The men who create power make an indispensable contribution to the nation's greatness, but the men who question power make a contribution just as indispensable, especially when that questioning is disinterested, for they determine whether we use power or power uses us.

Remarks at Amherst College, Amherst, Massachusetts,
October 26, 1963

It is regrettable that the gap between the intellectual and the politician seems to be growing. Instead of synthesis, clash and discord now characterize the relations between the two groups much of the time. Authors, scholars and intellectuals can praise every aspect of American society but the political. My desk is flooded with books, articles and pamphlets criticizing Congress. But rarely, if ever, have I seen any intellectual bestow praise on either the political profession or any political body for its accomplishments, its ability or its integrity—much less for its intelligence....

Both sides in this battle, it seems to me, are motivated by largely unfounded feelings of distrust. The politician, whose authority rests upon the mandate of the popular will, is resentful of the scholar who can, with dexterity, slip from position to position without dragging the anchor of public opinion.... The intellectual, on the other hand, finds it difficult to accept the differences between the laboratory and the legislature. In the former, the goal is truth, pure and simple, without regard to changing currents of public opinion; in the latter, compromises and majorities and procedural customs and rights affect the ultimate decision as to what is right or just or good.

And even when they realize this difference, most intellectuals consider their chief functions that of the critic—and politicians are sensitive to critics, possibly because we have so many of them.

Commencement address at Harvard University,
Cambridge, Massachusetts, June 14, 1956

If more politicians knew poetry and more poets knew politics, I am convinced that the world would be a little better place to live.

Ibid.

A healthy democratic political system rests on the ability of the electorate to know, understand and judge the attitudes, characteristics, opinions and qualifications of candidates for public office. Clearly political campaigns are essential to a democracy.

But the means by which they are financed have troubled thoughtful observers of the political scene for generations, and the concern has been nonpartisan.

The question posed by President Theodore Roosevelt about the propriety of public officeholders being obligated, if only morally, to a comparatively few large campaign contributors is equally pertinent today.

Our present system of financing political campaigns is deficient in that it does not ensure that candidates, or the parties they represent will have sufficient funds to provide adequate exposure to the electorate, and it has not effectively encouraged small contributions from a very large number of individuals.

> Letter to Congress on campaign costs, April 30, 1963

What can I do for you?

> Comment to Massachusetts voter during 1946
> congressional campaign

Presidents and Politics

The president of the United States, as Harry Truman has pointed out on many occasions, wears many hats, and one of them is the hat of the leader of his party.

> Remarks at dinner for Ohio governor Michael DiSalle,
> Columbus, January 6, 1962

The presidency has been called a good many names, and presidents have been also, but no president can do anything without the help of friends.

> Remarks at the Houston Coliseum,
> Houston, Texas, November 21, 1963

The presidency is not a very good place to make new friends.

> Press conference, December 12, 1962

Well, there's obviously a great interest in foreign policy, but I've attempted and I think this has been true of General [Dwight] Eisenhower in his campaign speeches, neither of us have attempted to make any partisan issue particularly out of foreign policy. There may be some areas of difference, but I think that those should be discussed as much as possible in a nonpolitical way because they involve the security of our country—where we differ, where the Republicans and Democrats differ.

> Interview with William Lawrence of ABC for
> the television program "Politics '62," October 14, 1962

My father is conservative. We disagree on many things. He's an isolationist and I'm an internationalist....I've given up arguing with him. But I make up my own mind and my own decisions.

> Interview with journalist Martin Papers, 1960

Look, Mr. Chairman [Nikita Khrushchev], you aren't going to make a communist out of me and I don't expect to make a capitalist out of you, so let's get down to business.

> Comment to Soviet Premier Nikita Khrushchev,
> Vienna, Austria, June 4, 1961

Most businessmen are Republicans...[and] have voted Republican in every presidential election. But that is not the important point—whether there is political agreement.

The important point is that they recognize and the government recognizes, and every group recognizes the necessity of attempting to work out economic policies which will maintain our economy at an adequate rate of growth. That is the great problem for us.

> Press conference, June 14, 1962

The trouble is, we are violating the Geneva agreement. Not as much as the North Vietnamese are, but we're violating it. Whatever we have to do, we have to do in some kind of secrecy, and there's a lot of danger in that. The Republicans want it both ways in Vietnam, and that's the privilege of the party not in power.... Now the Republicans want us to defeat communism by any means, but when we try to do it quietly, they howl that they're not being kept informed and that just means we are not doing enough.

> Comment to friends after dinner while watching TV in the
> White House, February 14, 1962

You can't get 66⅔ percent of the American people to agree on anything. And as for Congress, they're impossible. Ever since [Franklin D.] Roosevelt's day all the laws have been pretty much written downtown, and all the Senate investigations and hearings don't amount to much.

> Conversation with Benjamin Bradlee of
> *Newsweek*, May 21, 1963

CHAPTER 14

Insights on American Government

John Kennedy saw government and public service as vitally linked. In particular, he regarded a humane government as essential to balance against the power of business. After eight years of Republican rule, he anticipated a bureaucracy that would be hostile to Democratic-proposed change. By his inauguration, the size of the federal government had been spiraling upward for decades due to the vast programs and services launched during the Depression and World War II. The postwar period brought new governmental initiatives as well.

Like most centrists of his generation—the so-called "greatest generation"—Kennedy believed in the ability of centralized government to solve national problems. Aware of the difficulties ahead, even before the 1960 election, he solicited advice regarding the transition, including recommendations on how the new president should interact with Congress, the National Security Council, and Cabinet departments. He proposed new agencies including the Peace Corps and a Cabinet-level Department of Urban Affairs and Housing, as well as offering plans to reorganize major arms of the government. There were, for example, proposals to restructure the Securities and Exchange Commission that his father had chaired during the New Deal, the National Labor Relations Board, and the Federal Communications Commission.

The Role of Government

The federal government is not a remote bureaucracy.

Press conference, April 19, 1963

We properly establish high standards for our public servants. We investigate their character and associations before considering them for employment. We hire them only after they have passed difficult examinations. We require them to abide by rigorous standards of conduct and ethics. We demand consistently high performance from them on the job.

Message to Congress on federal pay reform, February 20, 1962

Improprieties occur in a good many different kinds of life, whether it's labor, management, or government. Not all people are able to withstand these pressures. But we intend that the personnel of the United States government will meet the highest ethical standards possible, and when they do not, action will be taken. My experience is that the great, great majority of them do. They are not paid very highly in most cases. They are dealing with matters of vital concern, and I think on the whole they do a good job. When they don't, it is most unfortunate and most regrettable, because all of us want the federal service to be of the highest possible standards.

Press conference, May 17, 1962

We have to get this country moving again.

Campaign line, 1960

No responsibility of government is more fundamental than the responsibility of maintaining the highest standards of ethical behavior by those who conduct the public business. There can be no dissent from the principle that all officials must act with unwavering integrity, absolute impartiality and complete devotion to the public interest.

This principle must be followed not only in reality but in appearance. For the basis of effective government is public confidence, and that confidence is endangered when ethical standards falter or appear to falter.
> Message to Congress on conflict of interest and problems of ethics in government, April 27, 1961

I don't believe in big government, but I believe in effective governmental action, and I think that's the only way that the United States is going to maintain its freedom. It's the only way that we're going to move ahead.... I think we're going to have to do a better job if we are going to meet the responsibilities which time and events have placed upon us.
> Debate with Vice President Richard Nixon, Chicago, September 26, 1960

I think it is too often that the government work has been caricatured rather than honored as it should be.
> Remarks on the Rockefeller Public Service Awards, December 6, 1962

The whole history of the world, from the struggle of the Athenians against the Macedonians to the experience of the British before World War II, in their competition with the Nazis, all show that for a free society to survive, to successfully compete, the leaders have to tell the truth. They have to be informed. They have to share their information with the people.
> Campaign remarks, University of California, Los Angeles, November 1, 1960

The federal government is the people, and the budget is a reflection of their need.
> Address to the American Society of Newspaper Editors, New York, April 19, 1963

From time to time statements are made labeling the federal government an outsider, an intruder, an adversary. In any free federation of states, of course, differences will arise and difficulties will persist.

But the people of this area know that the United States government is not a stranger or not an enemy. It is the people of 50 states joining in a national effort to see progress in every state of the Union....

Without the national government, the people of the United States, working together, there would be no protection of the family farmer, his income and his financial independence. For he would never have been able to electrify his farm, to insure his crop, to support its price and to stay ahead of the bugs, the boll weevils and the mortgage bankers.

>Remarks on the 30th Anniversary of the Tennessee Valley
>Authority, Muscle Shoals, Alabama, May 18, 1963

Rash talk is cheap, particularly on the part of those who do not have the responsibility.

>Press conference, September 13, 1962

The indestructible union of indestructible states, created by the Constitution, has been envied and imitated by many other nations. It is the best system yet devised. But we have to make it work. It has to have constant attention.

>Remarks to the National Conference of State Legislative Leaders,
>September 21, 1963

Responsible Americans are increasingly concerned with the widespread failure of our citizens to exercise their right to vote and restrictions which prevent many Americans from voting.

>Statement on the Commission on Registration and
>Voting Participation, March 30, 1963

[Washington, D.C.] is an artificial city, a governmental city, and well removed by design from a good many of the influences and pressures of ordinary life which you deal with on every occasion.

>Press conference, September 26, 1962

I have tried to make the whole tone and thrust of this office and this administration one that will demand a higher standard of excellence from every individual in his private life—in his education, his physical fitness, his attitudes toward foreign visitors, his obligations as a citizen, and all the rest.

> Letter to Alicia Patterson, editor and publisher of *Newsday*,
> May 16, 1961

And I can think of nothing more beneficial for those of us who work in Washington, in the nation's capital, than to leave on occasions and come out and see the people of the United States.

> Remarks at the dedication of the Oahe Dam, Pierre, South Dakota,
> August 17, 1962

A great mass of people frequently are not heard or may not be informed, may not understand the arguments, may feel the arguments are too complicated, may be so involved in their own private lives that they don't have time to take an informed interest in world events or in great national issues.

Therefore, the field is left to a few participants on both sides. I think that the wider we can spread this debate, the better off we will be.

> Interview with Robert Stein of *Redbook* magazine, August 1, 1963

I don't want to wake up on November 9 [Election Day] and have to ask myself, "What in the world do I do now?"

> Comment to advisor Clark Clifford, August 1960

I simply cannot afford to have just one set of advisors.

> Quoted in Richard Rovere, "Letter from Washington,"
> *The New Yorker*, December 24, 1960

It is much easier to make the speeches than it is to finally make the judgments, because unfortunately your advisors are frequently divided. If you take the wrong course, and on occasion I have, the president bears the burden of the responsibility quite rightly. The advisors may move on to new advice.

> Broadcast interview, "After Two Years—a Conversation
> with the President," December 17, 1962

It is an old argument when a case [against a new governmental policy] is lost to argue that it is all right here, but what is it going to mean for the future? That doesn't seem to me to be a rational argument. It was the kind of argument which was successfully defeated on many occasions during the administration of Franklin D. Roosevelt.

Press conference, March 21, 1962

I hope you will examine our political structure, which is not perhaps the most efficient in the world. And indeed it was developed in a sense to be inefficient in order to protect the rights of the individual. Winston Churchill once said that democracy is the worst form of government, except for all of the other systems that have been tried. It is among the most difficult.

Remarks to World Youth Forum delegates, March 7, 1963

How Government Works

I think that there are a lot of satisfactions to the presidency, particularly, as I say, we are all concerned as citizens and as parents and all the rest, with all the problems we have been talking about tonight. They are all the problems which, if I was not the president, I would be concerned about as a father or as a citizen.

Broadcast interview, "After Two Years—a Conversation with the President," December 17, 1962

The fact is, you can't carry out any policy without causing major frictions.

Press interview, Palm Beach, Florida, December 31, 1962

It is a tremendous change to go from being a senator to being president. In the first months, it is very difficult. The fact is, I think, that Congress looks more powerful sitting here than it did when I was there in the Congress. But that is because when you are in Congress, you are one of a hundred in the Senate or one of 435 in the House, so the power is divided. But from here I look at a Congress and I look at its collective power, particularly the bloc action, and it is a substantial power.

> Broadcast interview, "After Two Years—a Conversation with the President," December 17, 1962

When I was a congressman, I never realized how important Congress was, but now I do.

> Address to the Economic Club of New York, December 14, 1962

It is difficult for the average legislator to look far into the future; he is primarily concerned with the immediate problems.

> *Why England Slept,* 1940

The president bears particular responsibilities in the field of foreign policy. If there are failures in the Middle East, Africa, Latin America, and South Vietnam, it is usually not a senator who is selected to bear the blame, but it's the administration, the president of the United States.

> Press conference, November 14, 1963

We are so used to bringing about quick results in this country, of having decisions made and implemented, of having enemies overcome, of having questions declared critical and then attempted to be solved, that we perhaps are not always aware in the present encounter in which we are engaged how long must be our view, how patient we must be, how persevering we must be, and to recognize that there is no single action, no new dramatic policy, which can, of itself, and almost instantaneously, change basically the balance of events in our favor or make our lot and our way so much easier.

> Press conference, June 8, 1961

My experience in government is that when things are non-controversial, beautifully coordinated, and all the rest, it may be that there isn't much going on. I've never heard of any criticism of our organizational structure in several areas of the world which I know are rather inactive. So if you really want complete harmony and good will, then the best way to do it is not to do anything.

Press conference, June 28, 1961

You know that old story about Abraham Lincoln and the Cabinet. He says, "All in favor say, 'Aye,'" and the whole Cabinet voted aye, and then, "All opposed, 'No,'" and Lincoln voted no, and he said, "The vote is 'no.'"

Naturally, the Constitution places the responsibility on the president.

Broadcast interview "After Two Years—a Conversation with the President," December 17, 1962

I must say after being here for two years, there is no experience that you can get that can possibly prepare you adequately for the presidency.

Ibid.

They are two separate offices and two separate powers, the Congress and the presidency. There is bound to be conflict, but they must cooperate to the degree that is possible. But that is why no president's program is ever put in [quickly]. The only time it is put in quickly and easily is when the program is insignificant. But if it is significant and affects important interests and is controversial, therefore, then there is a fight, and the president is never wholly successful.

Ibid.

This Congress is somewhat like Lazarus. It has revived. It is moving.

Press conference, September 13, 1962

Congressmen are always advising presidents to get rid of presidential advisors. This is one of the most constant threads that runs through American history, and presidents ordinarily do not pay attention.

Press conference, May 8, 1963

I would not attempt to rank congressmen. What I am most interested in is the passage of legislation which is of benefit to the people.

Press conference, February 21, 1963

If you want to know my view, there is a difficulty between a Congress and a president, an executive. We are coordinate branches. There are different views, different interests. Perspectives are different from one end of Pennsylvania Avenue to the other. I've been fourteen times longer at one end of it than I have been at the other, so I appreciate the Congress' responsibilities.

Press conference, January 24, 1963

Any system of government will work when everything is going well. It's the system that functions in the pinches that survives.

Why England Slept, 1940

CHAPTER 15

Peace, War, and Terrorism

Born during World War I, John Kennedy was a leader whose worldview and politics were shaped by a relentless string of wars and threats of war. As a young man, he served as secretary to his father—the U.S. ambassador in London—and traveled in Europe while fascism and Nazism were amassing great power. Later, he wrote his Harvard honors thesis and a book about Britain's failure to assess accurately the huge threat posed by Nazi Germany.

During World War II, Kennedy overcame serious medical problems to enlist in the Navy, where he performed heroically as commander of PT 109 in the South Pacific. But the military crushing of Nazi Germany and expansionist Japan in 1945 brought no lasting world peace. Instead, it signaled the start of the Cold War in which the United States and Soviet Union—both heavily armed with conventional and nuclear weapons—fought for prestige, power, and spheres of influence globally and even in space. It was the era of the Korean War, of standoffs in a divided Germany, of tensions in Eastern Europe and Southeast Asia, of conflicts in the Middle East, and of communist control in China. Communist revolutionary movements succeeded in Cuba, Angola, and North Vietnam, among other places. Meanwhile, both blocs spent massive amounts of money on military endeavors, including weapons, aircraft, and submarines.

As international tensions rose amid fears of nuclear annihilation and terrorism, Kennedy sought to balance his advocacy of nuclear disarmament with a commitment to maintaining military strength, and his loathing for communism with a realistic understanding of the fragility of democracy. He therefore backed efforts to strengthen multinational institutions, from the United Nations—committed to peace—to the North Atlantic Treaty Organization and Southeast Asia Treaty Organization—preparing for potential war.

Initiatives for Peace and Cooperation

Peace and freedom do not come cheap, and we are destined, all of us here today, to live out most if not all of our lives in uncertainty and challenge and peril. Our policy must therefore blend whatever degree of firmness and flexibility which are necessary to protect our vital interests, by peaceful means if possible, by resolute action if necessary.

> Address at the University of North Carolina, Chapel Hill, October 12, 1961

Never was the desire for genuine understanding among the nations of the world stronger than today. The danger of ultimate disaster increases the urgency and need for a common cause of peace. Our people must lead the way toward relief from oppression, hunger and despair so that all may share in the vision of a good and righteous life.

> Statement on the Jewish High Holy Days, September 14, 1962

Let both sides explore what problems unite us instead of belaboring those problems which divide us.

> Inaugural Address, January 20, 1961

The United States can take care of itself, but the United Nations system exists so that every nation can have the assurance of security. Any attempt to destroy this system is a blow aimed directly at the independence and security of every nation, large and small....

I am a strong believer in the United Nations, and while it is possible to say they might interfere with some legitimate interests of ours in the near future, I am prepared to say that their actions in the past, at present, and I believe in the future represent the legitimate common interest of all members of the United Nations.

Press conference, February 15, 1961

I would be very unhappy if the United Nations were weakened or eliminated. You would have a great increase in the chances of a direct confrontation in some place like the Congo between the great powers. It might involve the United States directly and perhaps the Soviet Union on the other side. The United Nations serves as a means of channeling these matters, on which we disagree so basically, in a peaceful way.

Press conference, March 21, 1962

You must understand that few of the important problems of our time have, in the final analysis, been finally solved by military power alone.

Commencement address at the U.S. Naval Academy,
Annapolis, Maryland, June 7, 1961

But wherever we are, we must all, in our daily lives, live up to the age-old faith that peace and freedom walk together....

While we proceed to safeguard our national interests, let us also safeguard human interests. And the elimination of war and arms is clearly in the interest of both.

Commencement Address at American University,
June 10, 1963

We arm, as [British Prime Minister] Winston Churchill said a decade ago, to parley, to make it possible for us through diplomatic means to maintain the peace of the world, to maintain our security and those who are associated with us.

Address to the American veterans of World War II,
August 23, 1962

Soberly and unremittingly this nation—but never this nation alone—has sought the doorway to effective disarmament into a world where peace is secure.

>   Remarks at the signing of the Nuclear Test Ban treaty,
>   October 7, 1963

There is every reason to believe that the balanced search for peace through diplomacy, military strength and economic progress will prevent nuclear war and perhaps in the years ahead reduce the risk under which we live today. We know from recent experience how real these risks are and in the years ahead we must face the fact that they may well increase if the control of nuclear weapons spreads to more nations and possibly less responsible hands.

>   Message to state civil defense directors, May 8, 1963

In establishing our Peace Corps we intend to make full use of the resources and talents of private institutions and groups. Universities, voluntary agencies, labor unions and industry will be asked to share in this effort—contributing diverse sources of energy and imagination—making it clear that the responsibility for peace is the responsibility of our entire society.

>   Statement on establishing the Peace Corps, March 1, 1961

As Winston Churchill said, "It is better to jaw, jaw than to war, war," and we shall continue to jaw, jaw, and see if we can produce a useful result [on negotiating access to Berlin].

>   Press conference, May 9, 1962

For in the development of this organization rests the only true alternative to war—and war appeals no longer as a rational alternative. Unconditional war can no longer lead to unconditional victory. It can no longer serve to settle disputes. It can no longer concern the great powers alone....Mankind must put an end to war, or war will put an end to mankind....

And men may no longer pretend that the quest for disarmament is a sign of weakness—for in a spiraling arms race, a nation's security may well be shrinking even as its arms increase.

> Address to the United Nations General Assembly,
> New York, September 25, 1961

If this planet is ever ravaged by nuclear war—and if the survivors of that devastation can then endure the fire, poison, chaos and catastrophe—I do not want one of those survivors to ask another, "How did it all happen?" and to receive the incredible answer: "Ah, if one only knew."

> Comment to White House staff, 1962

It takes two to make peace. I think it would be misleading to suggest that there are some magic formulas hitherto untried which would ease the relations between the free world and the communistic world, or which would shift the balance of power in our favor.

> Comment to historian and biographer James MacGregor Burns,
> 1959

But peace cannot be brought about by concentrating solely on measures to control and eliminate weapons. It must also encompass measures to sustain and strengthen international institutions and the rule of law. A disarmament program must take into account the national security, our foreign policy, the relationships of this country to international peace-keeping agencies including the United Nations and our domestic and other policies. It should drive toward the creation of a peaceful world society in which disarmament, except for the forces needed to apply international sanctions, is the approved condition of international life.

> Letter to Congress proposing a U.S. Disarmament Agency,
> June 29, 1961

We live in a world, in short, where the principal problems that we face are not susceptible to military solutions alone.

The role of our military power, in essence, is, therefore, to free ourselves and our allies to pursue the goals of freedom without the danger of enemy attack, but we do not have a separate military policy, and a separate diplomatic policy, and a separate disarmament policy and a separate foreign aid policy. They are all bound up together in the policy of the United States. Our goal is a coherent, overall, national security policy, one that truly serves the best interests of the country and those who depend on it.

> Commencement address at the U.S. Air Force Academy,
> Colorado Springs, June 5, 1963

No generation is passed—no generation is passed without a war. War has taken up most of the time of the human race, and now we have the terrible responsibility, at a time when we have weapons which will destroy the human race, of working out means of living together.

That is a difficult task, and that is what you should spend your life, along with pursuing your own private interests—that is what we hope you will spend your life doing.

> Remarks to American Field Service students, July 18, 1963

For we do not intend to leave it to others to choose and monopolize the forum and the framework of discussion. We do not intend to abandon our duty to mankind to seek a peaceful solution.

> Report to the American people on the Berlin crisis, July 25, 1961

If we are to have peace between systems with far-reaching ideological differences, we must find ways for reducing or removing the recurring waves of fear and suspicion which feed on ignorance, misunderstanding or what appear to one side or the other as broken agreements. To me, the element of assurance is vital to the broader development of peaceful relationships.

> Letter on nuclear testing to Nikita Khrushchev, January 20, 1963

I believe our people have a right to expect to be led and not followed by their government in matters of national defense.

> Message to state civil defense directors,
> May 8, 1963

I think it is of the utmost importance that the heads of government of the major nuclear powers assume a personal responsibility for directing their countries' participation in and following the course of these [disarmament] negotiations.

> Message to Nikita Khrushchev concerning disarmament
> negotiations, February 25, 1962

We are ready and anxious to cooperate with all who are prepared to join in genuine dedication to the assurance of a peaceful and more fruitful life for all mankind.

> Greetings to leaders of the Soviet Union, January 21, 1961

The people of the United States and world stand at the crossroads. What we do now will shape the history of civilization for many years to come. We have a weary world trying to bind up the wounds of a fierce struggle. That is dire enough.

What is infinitely far worse is that we have a world which has unleashed the terrible power of atomic energy. We have a world capable of destroying itself.

The days which lie ahead are most difficult ones.

Above all, day and night, with every ounce of ingenuity and industry we possess, we must work for peace. We must not have another war.

> Congressional campaign radio broadcast, 1946

War is not our objective. Peace is our objective, along with our national security and the national security of those allied with us.

> Interview with Robert Stein of *Redbook* magazine, August 1, 1963

The Nuclear Test Ban Treaty will enable all of us who inhabit the earth, our children and children's children, to breathe easier, free from the fear of nuclear test fallout. It will curb the spread of nuclear weapons to other countries, thereby holding out hope for a more peaceful and stable world. It will slow down the arms race without impairing the adequacy of this nation's arsenal or security, and it will offer a small but important foundation on which a world of law can be built.

> Press conference, September 12, 1963

The task of building the peace lies with the leaders of every nation, large and small. For the great powers have no monopoly on conflict or ambition.

The Cold War is not the only expression of tension in this world—and the nuclear race is not the only arms race. Even little wars are dangerous in a nuclear world.

The long labor of peace is an undertaking for every nation—and in this effort none of us can remain unaligned. To this goal none can be un-committed.

> Address to the United Nations General Assembly,
> September 20, 1963

Threats and Horrors of War and Terrorism

Because of the ingenuity of science and man's own inability to control his relationships one with another, we happen to live in the most dangerous time in the history of the human race.

> Press conference, October 11, 1961

We must face the truth that people have not been horrified by war to a sufficient extent to force them to go to any extent rather than have another war.... War will exist until that distant day when the conscientious objector enjoys the same reputation and prestige that the warrior does today.

> Letter to a former World War II shipmate, 1945

Some years ago I visited the Polish cemetery near Cassino (in Italy), where thousands of Polish soldiers died far from their country in World War II for the independence of their country, and on that cemetery are written these words: "These Polish soldiers, for your freedom and theirs, have given their bodies to the soil of Italy, their hearts to Poland and their souls to God."

> Remarks at the Pulaski Day parade, Buffalo, New York,
> October 14, 1962

Guns and money are not the Middle East's basic need.

> Address to the Brotherhood Week observance of the National
> Conference of Christians and Jews,
> Cleveland, Ohio, February 24, 1957

The Free World's security can be endangered not only by a nuclear attack, but also by being slowly nibbled away at the periphery, regardless of our strategic power, by forces of subversion, infiltration, intimidation, indirect or non-overt aggression, internal revolution, diplomatic blackmail, guerilla warfare, or a series of limited wars.

> Message to Congress on the defense budget, March 18, 1961

We may again find ourselves with the Soviet Union toe to toe, but we ought to know what we have in our hands before we ask our allies to come with us to the brink again.

> Press conference, February 7, 1963

Our own strategic missiles have never been transferred to the territory of any other nation under a cloak of secrecy and deception; and our history—unlike that of the Soviets since the end of World War II—demonstrates that we have no desire to dominate or conquer any other nation or impose our system upon its people.

Nevertheless, American citizens have become adjusted to living daily on the bull's-eye of Soviet missiles located inside the U.S.S.R. or in submarines.

In that sense, missiles in Cuba add to an already clear and present danger—although it should be noted the nations of Latin America have never previously been subjected to a potential nuclear threat.

But this secret, swift and extraordinary buildup of communist missiles—in an area well known to have a special and historic relationship to the United States and the nations of the Western Hemisphere, in violation of Soviet assurances and in defiance of American and hemispheric policy—this sudden, clandestine decision to station strategic weapons for the first time outside of Soviet soil—is a deliberately provocative and unjustified change in the status quo which cannot be accepted by this country, if our courage and our commitments are ever to be trusted again by either friend or foe.

> Report to the American people on the Soviet arms buildup in
> Cuba, October 22, 1962

Mr. [Soviet Premier Nikita] Khrushchev does not wish us well, unfortunately.

> Broadcast interview, "After Two Years—a Conversation with the
> President," December 17, 1962

As Americans know from our history, on our old frontier, gun battles are caused by outlaws, and not by officers of the peace.

Terror is not a new weapon. Throughout history it has been used by those who could not prevail either by persuasion or example. But inevitably they fail, either because men are not afraid to die for a life worth living, or because the terrorists come to realize that free men cannot be frightened by threats and that aggression would meet its own response.

> Address to the United Nations General Assembly, New York,
> September 25, 1961

There is great difficulty in fighting a guerilla war. You need ten to one, or eleven to one, especially in terrain as difficult as in South Vietnam.

> Press conference, December 12, 1962

This most ancient form of [guerilla] warfare, going back as it has to its earliest beginnings, has become far more important than it has ever been in the past, and it is going to become more important in the future. As the great weapons become more deadly and as more and more nations possess them, there will be, of course, as has been very clearly pointed out by those who make themselves our adversaries, more and more emphasis on this kind of war, insurgency, guerilla, and the other kind of struggle, the so-called wars of liberation.

So that as the thermonuclear weapons get higher and higher in their megatonnage, and as there becomes less and less occasion to use them, then of course there will be more and more emphasis on this kind of struggle.

> Remarks at the Foreign Service Institute, July 3, 1962

One mistake can make this whole [world] blow up. One mistake either by Mr. [Soviet Premier Nikita] Khrushchev or by us here. I think anyone who looks at the fatality lists on atomic weapons, and realizes that the Communists have a completely twisted view of the United States, and that we don't comprehend them—that is what makes life in the sixties hazardous.

Broadcast interview, "After Two Years—a Conversation with the President," December 17, 1962

Cuba was the first time that the United States and the Soviet Union directly faced each other with the prospect of the use of military forces being used...which could possibly have escalated into a nuclear struggle. That is an important fact.

Ibid.

It was early in the Seventeenth Century that Francis Bacon [the Renaissance author and father of deductive reasoning] remarked on three recent inventions already transforming the world: the compass, gunpowder and the printing press. Now the links between the nations first forged by the compass have made us all citizens of the world, the hopes and threats of one becoming the hopes and threats of us all. In that one world's efforts to live together, the evolution of gunpowder to its ultimate limit has warned mankind of the terrible consequences of failure.

Address to the American Newspaper Publishers Association, New York, New York, April 27, 1961

With all the history of war, and the human race's history unfortunately has been a good deal more war than peace, with nuclear weapons distributed all through the world, and available, and with the strong reluctance of any people to accept defeat, I see the possibility in the 1970s of the president of the United States having to face a world in which fifteen or twenty or twenty-five of these nations may have these weapons. I regard that as the greatest possible danger and hazard.

Press conference, March 21, 1963

In an age when both sides have come to possess enough nuclear power to destroy the human race several times over, the world of communism and the world of free choice have been caught up in a vicious circle of conflicting ideology and interest. Each increase of tension has produced an increase of arms. Each increase of arms has produced an increase of attention.

Address on the Nuclear Test Ban treaty, July 26, 1963

Each day we draw nearer the hour of maximum danger, as weapons spread and hostile forces grow stronger.... The tide of events has been running out and time has not been our friend.... We cannot escape our dangers—neither must we let them drive us into panic or narrow isolation.... There will be further setbacks before the tide is turned. But turn it must. The hopes of mankind rest upon us.

State of the Union Address, January 30, 1961

Peace Through Strength

Above me is the Seal of the President of the United States, and in my State of the Union address, I called attention to the fact that the American eagle holds in its right hand the olive branch of peace and he holds in his left hand a bundle of arrows. I said in my State of the Union address that we intended to give equal attention to both—and we intend to do so.

Address to the Democratic Party of Cook County, Chicago, April 28, 1961

We are prepared to go any distance in order to maintain the peace, providing it does not involve the breaking of any commitments of the United States or involve any diminishment of the basic national security of the country.

Press conference, May 9, 1962

I wholly disagree with those who would put all their faith in an arms race and abandon their efforts for disarmament. But I equally disagree with those who would allow us neglect of our defensive needs in the absence of effective agreements for controlled disarmament.

Press conference, February 7, 1962

Strong words alone, of course, do not make meaningful policy; they must, in foreign affairs in particular, be backed both by a will and by weapons that are equally strong.

Introduction to *To Turn the Tide*, 1962

I believe in a strong America as the greatest defender of freedom. But I have never believed that making strong speeches means a strong country.

Remarks at Kentucky State Fairgrounds, Louisville, October 13, 1962

Ordinarily, military leaders are extremely reluctant to accept innovations. They continue with their old accepted techniques and methods.

Why England Slept, 1940

The Soviet Union tested [nuclear weapons] while we were at the negotiating table with them. If they fooled us once, it's their fault. If they fool us twice, it's our fault.

We would never test for political or psychological reasons, but only if we felt that the security of the United States was endangered, and therefore the free world, which does affect this generation and others to come. So we must balance off our risks.

Press conference, November 8, 1961

I think we should realize—as anyone who has studied the history of alliances—how enormous a task it is to have fifteen countries [in the North Atlantic Treaty Organization] moving down a stream all together over an issue which involves the security of them all.

Press conference, July 19, 1961

You've obviously seen on two occasions, when war broke out in Europe, there was some question of what the ultimate attitudes of the United States would be. NATO does not leave that in question. NATO guarantees. So this is the important defense for Europe and for us, and every evidence I have is that Europeans wish that to continue. Now, the day may come when their power is such that they can proceed on their defense without the United States, and no one in the United States that I know of wishes to stay a moment longer than our presence is desired or desirable.

Press conference, May 17, 1962

Our great asset is a willingness and a determination to fight through. Whether that spirit will stand through the kind of war we may have to embark on soon remains to be seen.

February 1942

This nation can afford to be strong—it cannot afford to be weak. We shall do what is needed to make and to keep us strong.

We must, of course, take advantage of every opportunity to reduce military outlays as a result of scientific or managerial progress, new strategic concepts, a more efficient, manageable and thus more effective defense establishment, or international agreements for the control and limitation of arms.

But we must not shrink from additional costs where they are necessary.

Message to Congress on the defense budget, March 28, 1961

We are amply strong for today and tomorrow, but we must consider the future too.

Press conference, February 7, 1962

When we are strong and when we are first, then freedom gains. Then the prospect for peace increases. Then the prospects for our society gain.

Debate with Vice President Richard Nixon, New York,
October 21, 1960

Postponement of practical measures to shield our people from fallout radiation cannot be justified by the inevitable imponderables and the continuing need for a greater research effort.

Letter to Congress on civil defense, August 3, 1962

The United States has the means as a sovereign power to defend itself. And of course exercises that power, has in the past, and would in the future. We would hope to exercise it in a way consistent with our treaty obligations, including the United Nations Charter. But we, of course, keep to ourselves and hold to ourselves under the United States Constitution and under the laws of international law, the right to defend our security on our own, if necessary. We hope to always move in concert with our allies—but on our own if that situation was necessary to protect our survival or integrity or other vital interests.

Press conference, November 20, 1962

My own feeling is that the military strength of the United States and the willingness of devoted Americans to serve this country all around the globe has played a major role in maintaining the rather uneasy peace of the last eighteen years.

Remarks to visitors from Brazilian military schools,
August 27, 1963

No matter how complicated war has now become, we need a Navy which can take ships in close to shore. We need an Air Force that can protect those ships. We need small boats that can take men on a beach. And we need men who will go ashore.

Remarks following inspection of the Marine barracks,
July 12, 1962

CHAPTER 16

International Affairs and Foreign Relations

John Kennedy was a "Cold Warrior" who saw conflicts between two diametrically opposed ideologies: communism and democracy. The actual battlefields scattered across the globe were military, diplomatic, economic, and philosophical. He mixed the rhetoric of idealism with hard pragmatism.

When he became president, many bitter wounds of World War II remained unhealed, including mistrust between France and Germany. Germany and Berlin remained divided, and communist regimes ruled Eastern and Central Europe. The Korean War was even fresher in American minds, leaving the southern part of the peninsula protected by a heavy contingent of U.S. troops; the threat of Chinese communism also loomed large in the American psyche. Communist movements fomented revolution in Africa and in Latin America. Middle East tensions were high between Israel and Arab nations. And it was a time when the United Nations was regarded optimistically as a great force for peace.

Meanwhile, Kennedy fertilized the seeds of war that the Eisenhower administration had sown in Southeast Asia, a war that would escalate after his assassination and that would plague America for decades to come. He faced other crises too, including the facedown over Soviet missiles in Cuba and the botched Bay of Pigs invasion of Cuba, led by U.S.-supported Cuban exiles.

In August 1961, the communists built a wall across Berlin, and two years later, Kennedy traveled there to proclaim: "All free men, wherever they may live, are citizens of Berlin, and, therefore, as a free man, I take pride in the words 'Ich bin ein Berliner.'" But as Kennedy well knew, international involvement was impossible without support at home. He launched the Peace Corps to build bridges between idealistic American volunteers and developing countries that had the option of turning to either Moscow or Washington, D.C., for assistance, and he proposed the Alliance for Progress as an avenue for "peaceful revolution" in Latin America. He promoted foreign aid not only for humanitarian reasons and to improve America's image overseas but also to help American farmers and corporations sell their products.

America's Role in the World

The United States, as all of you know, lived a life of comparative isolation for so many years, until the end of the Second World War.
> Remarks at the U.S. Embassy, Bad Godesberg, Germany,
> June 23, 1963

We must reject oversimplified theories of international life—the theory that American power is unlimited, or that the American mission is to remake the world in the American image. We must seize the vision of a free and diverse world—and shape our policies to speed progress toward a more flexible world order.
> Speech at the University of California at Berkeley,
> March 23, 1962

Whenever the United States has a disagreement with a foreign country, I think it's a mistake to assume that the United States is always wrong.
> Press conference, February 14, 1963

What kind of peace do we seek? Not a Pax Americana enforced on the world by American weapons of war. Not the peace of the grave or the security of the slave. I am talking about genuine peace, the kind of peace that makes life on earth worth living, the kind that enables men and nations to grow and to hope and to build a better life for their children—not merely peace for Americans but peace for all men and women—not merely peace for our time but peace for all times.

I speak of peace because of the new face of war. Total war makes no sense in an age when great powers can maintain large and relatively invulnerable nuclear forces and refuse to surrender without resort to those forces. It makes no sense in an age when a single nuclear weapon contains almost ten times the explosive force delivered by all of the allied air forces in the Second World War. It makes no sense in an age when the deadly poisons produced by a nuclear exchange would be carried by wind and water and soil and seed to the far corners of the globe and to generations yet unborn.

> Commencement address at American University, June 10, 1963

I think our people get awfully impatient and maybe fatigued and tired. They say, "We have been carrying this burden for seventeen years. Can we lay it down?"

We can't lay it down, and I don't see how we are going to lay it down in this century.

> Broadcast interview, "After Two Years—a Conversation with the President," December 17, 1962

Consider that the Asia-Pacific Triangle, as it is called, contains 50 percent of the world's population, and America 6 percent. Is it wise foreign policy for 6 percent to hold 50 percent in contempt?

> Address before the Washington chapter of the American Jewish Committee, June 4, 1957

I can well understand the attraction of those earlier days. Each one of us has moments of longing for the past, but two world wars have clearly shown us, try as we may, that we cannot turn our back on the world outside. If we do, we jeopardize our economic well-being, we jeopardize our political stability, we jeopardize our physical safety.

> Address at the Mormon Tabernacle, Salt Lake City, Utah, September 26, 1963

We do not desire to influence or dominate. What we desire to do is to see Europe and the United States together engaged in the struggle in other parts of the world. We cannot possibly survive if Europe and the United States are rich and prosperous and isolated. When success is in sight, we don't want to see this great partnership dissolved.

Press conference, January 24, 1963

Human nature is the same on both sides of the Iron Curtain.

Press conference, November 20, 1962

Geography has made us [Canada and the United States] neighbors. History has made us friends. Economics has made us partners. And necessity has made us allies. Those whom nature hath so joined together, let no man put asunder.

What unites us is far greater than what divides us. The issues and irritants that inevitably affect all neighbors are small indeed in comparison with the issues that we face together—above all the somber threat now posed to the whole neighborhood of this continent—in fact, to the whole community of nations. But our alliance is born, not of fear but of hope. It is an alliance that advances what we are for, as well as opposes what we are against.

Address to the Canadian Parliament, Ottawa, May 17, 1961

What we are anxious to do, of course, is protect our national security, protect the freedom of the countries, permit what Thomas Jefferson called the disease of liberty to be caught in areas which are now held by communists. We want to do that, of course, without having a nuclear war.

Now, if someone thinks we should have a nuclear war in order to win, I can inform them that there will not be winners in the next nuclear war, if there is one, and this country and other countries will suffer very heavy blows. So we have to proceed with responsibility and with care in an age where the human race can obliterate itself.

The objective of this administration, and I think the objective of the country, is to protect our security, keep the peace, protect our vital interests, make it possible for what we believe to be a system of government which is in accordance with the basic aspirations of people everywhere to ultimately prevail. That is our objective and that's the one we shall continue.

Press conference, February 14, 1962

On the whole, I think this country has done an outstanding job. A good many countries today are free that would not be free. Communism's gains since 1945 in spite of chaos and poverty have been limited, and I think the balance of powers still rests with the West, and I think it can increase our strength if we make the right decisions this year, economically here at home and in the field of foreign policy.

Interview with Chet Huntley and David Brinkley of NBC, September 9, 1963

This is one of the most serious, and I think in many ways stimulating problems we face: how to tell our story in a way that makes it new and exciting to young [foreign] students and also have them examine objectively under the light of present circumstances the serious failures of the Marxist system, which can be told from the Berlin Wall to China.

Press conference, February 21, 1962

The task of economic development is vital to the preservation of freedom in the turbulent, emerging continents of Asia, Africa and Latin America. It is also the duty which the strong owe to the weak.

Message to the Permanent Council of the North Atlantic Treaty Organization, February 15, 1961

But we have the will and the means to serve three related goals—the heritage of our countries, the unity of our continents and the interdependence of the Western alliance.

Some say the United States will neither hold to these purposes nor abide by its pledges—that we will revert to a narrow nationalism. But such doubts fly in the face of history.... The firmness of American will, and the effectiveness of American strength, have been shown, in support of free men and free government, in Asia, in Africa, in the Americas and, above all, here in Europe.

Address at the Paulskirche, Frankfurt, Germany, June 25, 1963

Africa's continuing march toward independence, unity and freedom—principles revered by the American people since the earliest days of our own nationhood—is a vital part of man's historic struggle for human dignity and self-realization.

Remarks to Conference of African Heads of State, May 22, 1963

We believe strongly in democracy and personal freedom, but I also strongly believe, and I think the other responsible leaders in this hemisphere strongly believe, that through a system of national sovereignty and personal independence and personal liberty we can best advance the interest of all our people.

Toast to the president of Chile, December 11, 1962

The United States is playing an increasingly significant role in the world today as the chief defender of freedom in a time of freedom's maximum danger. The entire democratic system which depends for its success upon majority rule, and therefore for majority understanding, depends in a very real sense on information and communication—for our judgment is no better than our information.

Remarks marking twenty-five years of *Life* magazine, March 2, 1961

The United States can never leave Europe. We are too much bound together.

Press interview, Palm Beach, Florida, December 31, 1962

For we seek not merely the welfare and equality of nations one with another—but the welfare and the equality of the people within our nations. In so doing we are fulfilling the most ancient dreams of the founders of this hemisphere, [George] Washington, [Thomas] Jefferson, [Simón] Bolívar, [José] Martí, [José de] San Martín and all the rest.

Address on the first anniversary of the Alliance for Progress, March 13, 1962

I regard Latin America as the most critical area in the world today, and I would hope that Western Europe and the United States would not be so preoccupied with our disputes—which historically may not seem justified—when we have a very, very critical problem which should concern us both in Latin America.

Press conference, February 7, 1963

In considering the problems in our own hemisphere, we have to remember that the United States is holding back—protecting—a good many countries which are in the direct line of hazard in the Middle East, in Asia, and in Western Europe—and that in itself is a substantial accomplishment.

We can assist these countries by our guarantees against outright military invasion. We can assist them through economic assistance to improve the life of their people. We can assist them through defense support in strengthening their armed forces against internal guerilla activity. But in the final analysis, they have to—and we cannot do it for them—organize the political and social life of the country in such a way that they maintain the support of their people.... [They must] identify their government with the people.

Press conference, May 5, 1961

The aims of the United Nations—as expressed in the Charter—are comparable to the aims of the United States as expressed in the Constitution. Both documents affirm ideas and principles which transcend partisanship.

When all nations adopt as their own—and conduct their affairs in accord with—the objectives of the United Nations Charter, our hopes and expectations for the world organization will be fulfilled.

Message to Congress on U.S. participation in the United Nations,
March 15, 1962

It is odd that this country, which was wholly founded in a long neutral tradition, and isolationist tradition, should, in 1962, as it has been since 1945, be the great and almost solitary hope for the maintenance of freedom around the world. Everything that we do to strengthen and develop our country means not only a better life for our own people, but also for those hundreds of millions who now stand and look to us and also look to the East.

Remarks at Kentucky State Fairgrounds, Louisville,
October 13, 1962

The peace-keeping machinery of the United Nations cannot work without the help of the smaller nations, nations whose forces threaten no one and whose forces can thus help create a world in which no nation is threatened. Great powers have their responsibilities, their burdens, but the smaller nations of the world must fulfill their obligations as well.

> Address to the Irish Parliament, Dublin,
> June 28, 1963

We must recognize that foreign policy in the modern world does not lend itself to easy, simple, black-and-white solutions. If we were to have diplomatic relations only with those countries whose principles we approved of, we would have relations with very few countries in a very short time. If we were to withdraw our assistance from all governments who are run differently from our own, we would relinquish the world immediately to our adversaries.

If we were to treat foreign policy as merely a medium for delivering self-righteous sermons to supposedly inferior people, we would give up all thought of world influence or world leadership.

For the purpose of foreign policy is not to provide an outlet for our own sentiments of hope or indignation; it is to shape real events in a real world. We cannot adopt a policy which says that if something does not happen, or others do not do exactly what we wish, we will return to "Fortress America." That is the policy in this changing world of retreat, not of strength.

> Speech at the Mormon Tabernacle, Salt Lake City, Utah,
> September 26, 1963

I know there are always some people who feel that Americans are always young and inexperienced, and foreigners are always able and tough and great negotiators. But I don't think that the United States would have acquired its present position of leadership in the free world if that view were correct.

> Press conference, January 31, 1962

Confronting Crisis, Challenge, and Change

This is a small world and becoming smaller every day. The cause of freedom is under challenge all over the globe.

> Remarks on the first C-141 all-jet transport, August 22, 1963

Today no war has been declared—and however fierce the struggle may be, it may never be declared in the traditional fashion. Our way of life is under attack. Those who make themselves our enemy are advancing around the globe. The survival of our friends is in danger. And yet no war has been declared, no borders have been crossed by marching troops, no missiles have been fired.

> Address to the American Newspaper Publishers Association,
> New York, April 27, 1961

It would be well to remind us all concerned of the hard and fast realities of this nation's relationship with Europe: realities of danger, power and purpose which are too deeply rooted in history and necessity to be either obscured or altered in the long run by personal or even national differences.

> Press conference, January 24, 1963

Two central weaknesses in our current foreign policy: first, a failure to appreciate how the forces of nationalism are rewriting the geopolitical map of our world...and second, a lack of decision and conviction in our leadership...which seeks to substitute slogans for solutions.

> "A Democrat Looks at Foreign Policy," *Foreign Affairs* magazine,
> October 1957

Dictatorships of the Left or Right are equally abhorrent, no matter what their doctrine or how great their efficiency.

> Diary entry, July 2, 1945

Abroad, the balance of power is shifting. There are new and more terrible weapons—new and uncertain nations—new pressures of population and deprivation. One-third of the world, it has been said, may be free—but one-third is the victim of cruel repression—and the other one-third is rocked by the pangs of poverty, hunger and envy. More energy is released by the awakening of these new nations than by the fission of the atom itself.

Meanwhile, communist influence has penetrated further into Asia, stood astride the Middle East and now festers some ninety miles off the coast of Florida. Friends have slipped into neutrality—and neutrals into hostility....

The world has been close to war before—but now man, who has survived all previous threats to his existence, has taken into his mortal hands the power to exterminate the entire species some seven times over.

> Democratic nomination acceptance speech,
> Los Angeles, July 15, 1960

These countries are passing through very difficult times and they're going to swing one way and then another. But in general, our object is that they maintain their independence. We hope it's theirs.

> Press conference, October 11, 1961

We are in a very changing period in the world—in fact, in all parts of the world—behind the Iron Curtain and indeed on this side of the Iron Curtain.

> Press conference, January 24, 1963

The regimentation and unification achieved by force and propaganda will give a dictator an initial jump on his opponents. However, we believe that a democracy can, by voluntary action, equal this effort when the emergency comes and sustain it over a longer period of time. We believe that groups will coordinate their private interests with national interest, thus giving a greater force and vigor than could have been attained by totalitarian methods.

> *Why England Slept*, 1940

These are the kinds of problems that we are dealing with. I said something about them yesterday: The use which the communists make of democratic freedoms and the success which they are able to—once they have seized power—success with which they are able to maintain their power against dissent....

How we fight that kind of problem which is going to be with us all through this decade seems to me to be one of the great problems now before the United States. And I would hope all those who are concerned about the advance of communism would face that problem and not concern themselves with the loyalty of President Eisenhower or President Truman or Mrs. [Eleanor] Roosevelt or myself or someone else.

Press conference, April 21, 1961

The forces in the world hostile to us are powerful. We went through a very difficult and dangerous experience this fall in Cuba. I have seen no real evidence that the policy of the communist world towards us is basically changed. They still do not wish us well. We are not yet in the harbor. We are still in very stormy seas.

Press conference, February 7, 1963

I'm sorry the Soviet Union is testing [nuclear weapons]. They broke the agreement and tested again last fall. We tested in response. Now they carry out another series of tests and the world plunges deeper into uncertainty.

Press conference, July 23, 1962

The big dangers to Latin America are the very difficult, and in some ways desperate, conditions in the countries themselves, unrelated to Cuba. Illiteracy, or bad housing, or maldistribution of wealth, or political or social instability—these are all problems we find [as well as] a diminishing exchange, balance-of-payments difficulties, and a drop in the price of their raw materials, upon which their income depends. These are all problems that are staggering, to which we ought to be devoting our attention.

Press conference, February 7, 1963

We know that the struggle between the communist system and ourselves will go on. We know it will go on in economics, in productivity, in ideology, in Latin America and Africa, in the Middle East and Asia.

Remarks at Yellowstone County Fairgrounds, Billings, Montana, September 25, 1963

The free world is entirely open to communist propaganda and argumentation, and we have no fear of engaging in a battle of ideas. But the communist world is largely closed to information and to Western thought and receives a one-sided view, not only of ideological matters but even of factual developments throughout the world.

> Statement on Radio Free Europe, October 25, 1963

[Soviet Premier Nikita] Khrushchev has compared the United States to a worn-out runner living on its past performance and stated that the Soviet Union would out-produce the United States by 1970.

Without wishing to trade hyperbole with the Chairman, I do suggest that he reminds me of the tiger hunter who has picked a place on the wall to hang the tiger's skin long before he has caught the tiger. The tiger has other ideas.

> Press conference, June 28, 1961

The American people admire the resolute spirit and manifest courage of the Turkish people in facing the trials of the postwar years and in their forthright attack on the problems of economic and social development which will determine Turkey's future.

> Message on the 40th anniversary of the Republic of Turkey,
> October 29, 1963

Quite obviously, the German people wish to be reunited. If the people of the United States had lost a struggle, and the Mississippi River divided us, we would wish to be reunited. I think the people of the Soviet Union, if they experienced a comparable fate, would wish to be reunited. People and families wish to join together. So that is the object of our policy.

> Press conference, June 24, 1963

We would agree that there is unfinished business to be settled as concerns Germany. For many years, the Western nations have proposed a permanent and peaceful settlement of such questions on the basis of self-determination of the German people.

Moreover, we shall always be ready to discuss any proposals which would give increased protection to the right of the people of Berlin to exercise their independent choice as free men.

The proposals which have now been placed before us move in the opposite direction and are so recognized throughout the world.

Discussions will be profitable if the Soviets will accept in Berlin, and indeed in Europe, self-determination which they profess in other parts of the world, and if they will work sincerely for peace rather than an extension of power.

Press conference, June 28, 1961

My concern is that the relationship between Europe and the United States be intimate. I'm hopeful that we can reach accommodations on the economic relations, of trade, and also the problem of currencies and all the rest, on the problem of military policy. Europe does not want to be dependent upon the United States, and we do not want that relationship. We meet as equals when this work is completed.

Press conference, July 5, 1962

While we all regret Pearl Harbor and everything else [from World War II], we are in a new era in our relations with Japan, fortunately.

Press conference, April 11, 1962

Peace does not come automatically from a "peace treaty." There is peace in Germany today even though the situation is "abnormal." A "peace treaty" that adversely affects the lives and rights of millions will not bring peace with it. A "peace treaty" that attempts to affect adversely the solemn commitments of three great powers will not bring peace with it. We again urge the Soviet government to reconsider its course, to return to the path of constructive cooperation it so frequently states it desires, and to work with its World War II Allies in concluding a just and enduring settlement of issues remaining from that conflict.

Press conference, July 19, 1961

The great battleground for the defense and expansion of freedom today is the whole southern half of the globe—Asia, Latin America, Africa and the Middle East—the lands of the rising peoples. Their revolution is the greatest in human history. They seek an end to injustice, tyranny and exploitation. More than an end, they seek a beginning.

And theirs is a revolution which we would support regardless of the Cold War, and regardless of which political or economic route they should choose to freedom.

For the adversaries of freedom did not create the revolution, nor did they create the conditions which compel it. But they are seeking to ride the crest of its wave—to capture it for themselves.

Message to Congress on urgent national needs, May 25, 1961

However much we may sympathize with [the Cubans'] desire to be free, the United States cannot launch itself into a massive invasion of Cuba without considering the worldwide implications to other free countries and also its effect upon our own position.

Response to question at the American Society of Newspaper Editors Conference, April 19, 1963

I've always felt, and I think history will record, that the change of China from being a country friendly to us to a country which is unremittingly hostile affected very strongly the balance of power in the world. And while there were—still is, of course—room for argument as to whether any United States actions would have changed the course of events there, I think a greater effort would have been wiser. I said it in 1949, so it isn't totally hindsight.

Press conference, November 29, 1961

I do not believe that meetings between heads of state, either allies or those whose purposes make them our adversaries, are designed to solve a series of specific problems or bring about a fundamental change in relationships. For only changes in the realities which underlie the relations between nations, shifts in power, the pressure of events, revisions of policies which reflect new needs, fresh assessments and the change in power balances within the countries—only such changes as these leave a permanent mark on the prospects for peace.

And while meetings of presidents and premiers can sometimes help in fulfilling such changes, they rarely initiate them.

Remarks at Democratic National Committee dinner, May 27, 1961

A summit is not a place to carry on negotiations which involve details. [Rather] a summit should be a place where perhaps agreements which have been achieved at a lower level could be finally, officially approved by the heads of government, or if there were a major crisis which threatened to involve us all in a war, there might be a need for a summit. But my general view would be that we should climb to the summit after careful preparation at the lower levels.

Press conference, February 14, 1962

Now, in our own time, the inter-American system faces old foes and new challenges; and it is again demonstrating the capacity for change which has always given it strength. The foes are stronger and more determined than ever before and the challenges are more difficult, more complex and more burdensome.

For today we are faced not merely with the protection of new nations, but with the remolding of ancient societies—not only with the destruction of political enemies, but with the destruction of poverty, hunger, ignorance and disease—not alone with the creation of national dignity but with the preservation of human dignity.

Address upon the opening of the Central American Presidents' Conference, San José, Costa Rica, March 18, 1963

The reconciliation of France and Germany is essential to the security of the West. Europe has been torn by civil wars over a good many hundreds of years. To end that prospect, to bring France and Germany together, is a matter of the greatest priority of the French and German people, and of the greatest interest to us.

Press conference, June 24, 1963

For more than ten years, [Radio Free Europe] has been reaching out to people in Eastern Europe: truth, devotion to liberty is its message. For this radio is at work, with listeners numbering in the millions. The competition of ideas in these countries is kept alive. Individual Americans by giving to Radio Free Europe may be sure that they are bringing a beacon of light into countries to which millions of us are tied by kinship, and whose hope for freedom all of us must share.

This is a peaceful concern but a firm one.

Press conference, March 8, 1961

Foreign Assistance

History records that our contributions to international aid have been the critical factor in the growth of a whole family of international financial institutions and agencies, playing an even more important role in the ceaseless war against want and the struggle for growth and freedom.

And, finally, history will record that today our technical assistance and development loans are giving hope where hope was lacking, sparking action where life was static and stimulating progress around the earth—simultaneously supporting the military security of the free world, helping to erect barriers against the growth of communism where those barriers count the most, helping to build the kind of world community of independent, self-supporting nations in which we want to live and helping to serve the deep American urge to extend a generous hand to those working toward a better life for themselves and their children.

Message to Congress on Free World defense and assistance
programs, April 2, 1963

No foreign aid program can and should substitute for private initiative, but it can assist in breaking the path.

Address at White House Conference on Exports,
September 17, 1963

Foreign aid—America's unprecedented response to world challenges—has not been the work of one party or one administration. It has moved forward under the leadership of two great presidents—Harry Truman and Dwight Eisenhower—and drawn its support from forward-looking members of both political parties in the Congress and throughout the nation.

Message to Congress on foreign aid, March 22, 1961

Our view of the world crisis is that countries are entitled to national sovereignty and independence. That is all we ever suggested. That is the purpose of our aid—to make it more possible.

Press conference, October 11, 1961

Foreign aid is not advanced only out of American economic self-interest. The gulf between rich and poor which divides the Family of Man is an invitation to agitators, subversives and aggressors. It encourages the ambition of those who desire to dominate the world, which threatens the peace and freedom of us all....

This is not a partisan matter.... Yet there are still those who are unable or unwilling to accept these simple facts—who find it politically convenient to denounce foreign aid on the one hand, and in the same sentence to denounce the communist menace....

Nearly two years ago my wife and I visited Bogotá, Colombia, where a vast new Alliance for Progress housing was just getting under way. Earlier this year I received a letter from the first resident of this 1,200 new home development. "Now," he wrote, " we have dignity *and* liberty."

Speech to the Protestant Council of the City of New York, November 8, 1963

I think that all of us who live in the prosperous areas of the West must make a concerted national and international effort to assist the people of the underdeveloped world—who have their political independence but who live on the marginal edge of existence in many cases—to move toward a better life. Because, if they feel they cannot do it under a system of freedom, then they will turn to a totalitarian system.

Interview recorded for French TV and radio, May 30, 1961

And unless we can adjust our affairs so that the power of the West is brought to bear on the great desperate areas of the world, particularly to the south of us, obviously we are going to fail. So the first job, the first priority, is to make sure that we are using all of our combined talents to provide for an easy flow back and forth of goods, services, that we are the masters of our monetary arrangements, not their servant. And then we can match our power against any combinations in the world.

Toast to Prince Albert of Belgium, February 26, 1963

The cause of freedom is under attack in many parts of the world and certainly its external enemies proceed with a good deal of vigor and strength. We also have internal enemies and those are poverty and illiteracy and disease. We attempt, together, to combat both of these enemies; abroad by building our strength, making clear our commitments, fulfilling those commitments, and at home we fight these internal enemies with the great concentrated social effort of your government, the effort of this government.

Remarks to the president of Honduras, November 30, 1962

In my lifetime, I had been present, alive, during three world wars, and it is impossible to study the origins of each of these struggles without realizing the serious miscalculations which were made by the leaders on both sides. The most recent example was Korea, where the North Koreans did not seem certain that we would respond immediately upon the occasion of their invasion into South Korea, and where there was serious doubt on the part of the United States that the Chinese communists would intervene as we moved to the north. In the experience of Europe, you have had the same circumstances.

Therefore, when responsibility is pressed heavily on anyone to make a judgment, it seems to me useful to have as close an understanding of the view of each side as possible. I think that it is most valuable to talk to those with whom we are allied. I also think it is important that we talk to those who are separated from us, because in the final analysis, heavy decisions rest, constitutionally upon the president of the United States.

Press conference, Paris, France, June 2, 1961

There are many things that happen in Eastern Europe, as I said in my United Nations speech, which we consider to be wholly unsatisfactory—

the denial of liberties, the denial of political freedom and national independence, and all the rest.

And that is a matter of equal concern in the action which you described [the building of the Berlin Wall]. These are areas which the Soviet Union has held since the end of World War II, for over sixteen years.

Press conference, October 11, 1961

CHAPTER 17

Celebrities and World Leaders

Raised in a socially prominent and politically involved family, John Kennedy was always comfortable—even as a Harvard student—socializing and talking with the powerful and the famous, from British aristocrats to chiefs of state and from stars of music, theater, and film to politicians with as much ambition and drive as himself. As his own political career advanced, movers and shakers from the United States and abroad were eager to meet with the handsome, intelligent, focused, and wealthy representative and senator. Of course, the presidency gave Kennedy an unparalleled forum for hosting renowned musicians, prime ministers, Nobel laureates, and royalty. He understood and used Americans' fascination with fame and glamour, observing in his 1940 book *Why England Slept,* "In this country, of course, great emphasis has always been placed on the individual. Personalities have always been more interesting to us than facts." And Kennedy's own keen interest in international affairs led to foreign trips where he spent time with world leaders. Thus, his assessments and insights about the celebrities of his era came from several vantage points, including personal meetings in official and social settings, from the lessons of contemporary history, and from the perspectives of his family and advisers.

Kennedy's comments were often diplomatic—such as when he publicly discussed visiting world leaders he disagreed with, mistrusted, or disliked. Yet he could be caustic about perceived enemies such as Cuban President Fidel Castro and Soviet leader Nikita Khrushchev. And as in the case of French President Charles de Gaulle, he could be generous in his public praise but sharp-tongued in private comments to his friends.

American Figures

Dwight D. Eisenhower (1890–1969) served as supreme commander of the Allied forces in Europe during World War II, became president of Columbia University, and preceded Kennedy as a two-term Republican president.

He never lost that humble way and therefore easily won the hearts of those with whom he worked.

Diary entry, June 30, 1945

William Faulkner (1897–1962), the South's best-known novelist, won the Nobel Prize in Literature in 1949.

Since Henry James, no writer has left behind such a vast and enduring monument to the strength of American literature.

His death came in Oxford, Mississippi, in the heart of the setting for that turbulent world of light and shadow which was the towering creation of his mind and art. From this world he sought to illuminate the restless searching of all men. And his insight spoke to the heart of all who listened.

A Mississippian by birth, an American by virtue of those forces and loyalties which guided his work, a guiding citizen of our civilization by virtue of his art. William Faulkner now rests, the search done, his place secure among the great creators of this age.

Statement on William Faulkner's death, July 6, 1962

Felix Frankfurter (1882–1965), a cofounder of the American Civil Liberties Union, was a Harvard Law School professor until his appointment to the U.S. Supreme Court in 1939.

You have been part of the American public life for well over half a century.

Letter on Frankfurter's retirement, August 29, 1962

New England poet Robert Frost (1874–1963) recited his poem, "The Gift Outright," at Kennedy's inauguration.

He was the great American poet of our time. His art and his life summed up the essential qualities of the New England he loved so much: the fresh delight in nature, the plainness of speech, the canny wisdom and the deep, underlying insight into the human soul. He had promises to keep, and miles to go, and now he sleeps.

Statement on Robert Frost's death, January 29, 1963

I knew Mr. Frost quite late in his life, in really the last four or five years, and I was impressed, as I know you were who knew him, by a good many qualities, but also by his toughness. He gives the lie, as a good many other poets have, to the fact that poets are rather sensitive creatures who live in the dark of the garret.

He was very hardboiled in his approach to life, and his desires for our country. He once said that America is the country you leave only when you want to go out and lick another country.

Remarks at the froundbreaking for the Robert Frost Library, Amherst, Massachusetts, October 26, 1963

Barry Goldwater (1909–1998), a conservative from Arizona, was the 1964 Republican nominee for president. A former member of the Phoenix City Council, he served in the Senate from 1953 to 1965 and again from 1969 to 1987.

The trouble is that if [Goldwater]'s the nominee, people will start asking him questions, and he's so damn quick on the trigger that he will answer them. And when he does, it will be all over.

> Conversation with Benjamin Bradlee of *Newsweek*, May 9, 1963

I really like him, and if we're licked at least it will be on the issue. At least the people will have a clear choice.

> Conversation with Benjamin Bradlee of *Newsweek*,
> November 5, 1963

Rev. Billy Graham (1918–), a conservative Protestant evangelist, counseled many presidents, Republican and Democratic alike.

He has, I think, transmitted this most important quality of our common commitments to faith in a way which makes all of us particularly proud.

> Remarks at the 10th Annual Presidential Prayer Breakfast,
> March 1, 1962

U.S. Representative Charlie Halleck (1900–1986) of Indiana was the Republican minority leader of the House of Representatives.

Trying to touch Charlie is like trying to pick up a greased pig.

> Conversation with Benjamin Bradlee of
> *Newsweek*, October 23, 1963

Novelist Ernest Hemingway (1899–1961), a one-time journalist, became one of America's most influential and widely read novelists and won a Nobel Prize for Literature.

Few Americans have had a greater impact on the emotions and attitudes of the American people than Ernest Hemingway. From his first emergence as one of the bright literary stars in Paris during the Twenties—as a chronicler of the "Lost Generation," which he was to immortalize—he almost single-handedly transformed the literature and the ways of thought of men and women in every country in the world.

When he began to write, the American artist had to look for a home on the Left Bank of Paris. Today, the United States is one of the great centers of art. Although his journeys throughout the world—to France, to Spain and even to Africa—made him one of the great citizens of the world, he ended life as he began it—in the heartland of America to which he brought renown and from which he drew his art.

> Statement on Hemingway's death, July 15, 1960

Jimmy Hoffa (1913–1975) was the president of the International Brotherhood of Teamsters who served a prison term for corruption and later disappeared in what many observers believe was a murder committed by organized crime.

I'm not satisfied when I see men like Jimmy Hoffa, in charge of the largest union in the United States, still free.

> Debate with Vice President Richard Nixon, Chicago,
> September 26, 1960

J. Edgar Hoover (1895–1972) was the powerful director of the Federal Bureau of Investigation from 1924 until his death.

Boy, the dirt he has on those senators.

> Conversation with Benjamin Bradlee of *Newsweek*,
> November 5, 1963

He's the biggest bore.

> Remark to advisor Kenneth O'Donnell March 1962

Robert McNamara (1916–), a former Ford Motor Co. executive, was secretary of Defense under both Kennedy and Lyndon B. Johnson, and then president of the World Bank from 1968 to 1981.

He's one of the few guys around this town who, when you ask him if he has anything to say and he hasn't, says "no." That's rare these days. I'm telling you.

> Phone call to Benjamin Bradlee of *Newsweek*, March 3, 1962

Richard Nixon (1913–1994), a former senator from California, was the Republican vice president when he narrowly lost to Kennedy in the 1960 election. He was elected president in 1968, reelected in 1972, and resigned to avoid impeachment in 1973.

He's a cheap bastard. That's all there is to it.

> Phone call to Benjamin Bradlee of *Newsweek*, April 10, 1962

For just as historians tell us that Richard I was not fit to fill the shoes of bold Henry II—and that Richard Cromwell was not fit to wear the mantle of his uncle—they might add in future years that Richard Nixon did not measure to the footsteps of Dwight D. Eisenhower.

> Democratic nomination acceptance speech,
> Los Angeles, July 15, 1960

George Romney (1907–1995) was governor of Michigan and former head of American Motors Corp. He was a contender for the 1964 Republican presidential nomination.

You have to be a little suspicious of somebody as good as Romney. No vices whatsoever, no smoking and no drinking. Imagine someone we know going for twenty-four or forty-eight hours to fast and meditate, awaiting a message from the Lord whether to run or not to run.

> Conversation with Paul Fay Jr., 1962

Eleanor Roosevelt (1884–1962) was the wife of President Franklin D. Roosevelt. After the death of her husband, she served as U.S. delegate to the United Nations, helped create the 1948 Universal Declaration of Human Rights, and championed the causes of social justice, equality, and world peace.

Mrs. Roosevelt lived in the White House longer than any other woman. She also made her experience in the White House a vivid one in that her influence spread far beyond its walls to all parts of the country and her identification was constant, her concern was permanent, for the great causes which were identified with her husband's life and which we identify with the best of America, concern for her fellow citizens, particularly those less fortunate.

> Remarks on signing legislation to create the Eleanor Roosevelt
> Foundation, April 23, 1963

Since the day I entered this office, she has been both an inspiration and a friend, and my wife and I always looked forward to her visits to the White House, to which she always lent such grace and vitality.

> Statement on Eleanor Roosevelt's death, November 7, 1962

In the time I have been here, she visited the White House on five or six occasions and on each of those occasions her visit was connected with some phase of her horizon-wide interest in life and in people. Each visit was connected with a different cause and each cause…was important to our country and to the world.

The things for which Mrs. Roosevelt stood are clearly identifiable and they represent the best of our national effort and purpose.

> Remarks on the Eleanor Roosevelt commemorative stamp,
> October 11, 1963

Margaret Chase Smith (1897–1995), a Maine Republican, served in the House and then in the Senate. She was the first woman whose name was placed in nomination for the presidency at a major political party nominating convention.

I think if I were a Republican candidate, I would not look forward to campaigning against Margaret Chase Smith in the New Hampshire presidential primary. She is very formidable, if that is the appropriate word to use about a very fine lady. She is a very formidable political figure.

Press conference, November 14, 1963

Adlai Stevenson (1900–1965) served as governor of Illinois, U.S. ambassador to the United Nations, and two-time unsuccessful Democratic nominee for president.

The force, eloquence and courage with which he has advanced the American viewpoint have played no small part in helping to confine these crises to the [United Nations Security] Council chambers, where they belong.

Preface to Adlai Stevenson's book *Looking Outward: Years of Crisis at the United Nations*, October 24, 1963

Adlai Stevenson is a bitter man. He's a bitter, deeply disillusioned, deeply hurt man.

Comment to journalist Peter Lisagor, 1960

Nuclear physicist Edward Teller (1908–2003) was a Hungarian refugee who became a major figure in America's development of the atomic and hydrogen bombs.

Dr. Teller was one of a number of Europeans who came to the United States and played a most significant role in World War II, and has contributed immeasurably to the security of the United States since that time.

I think we take a good deal of pride and satisfaction that our country was the magnet which attracted these free-ranging minds who, because of their great talent and ability to concentrate that talent on new horizons, were able to make some of the most remarkable breakthroughs in scientific history. And we are also glad to have him because he not only has been an innovator and an original researcher, but also a distinguished teacher.

Remarks on Presenting the Enrico Fermi Award to Edward Teller,
December 3, 1962

International Figures

Konrad Adenauer (1876–1967) was lord mayor of Cologne until ousted by the Nazis and served as chancellor of West Germany from 1949 until 1963.

You assumed the burdens of office at a most difficult and painful moment in the history of the German people—after long, hard years of dictatorship and devastating war. And to your people you have given, by your wise and responsible, leadership, a sense of national identity, purpose and pride.

Western Europe, prior to your service as chancellor, was still obsessed by bitter and traditional rivalries, hatreds and fears.... Germany today is respected by all free nations as a champion of peace and freedom—for you have created in your own land a stable, free and democratic society which stands in sharp contrast to the repression still enforced on so many of your countrymen....

Your place in history is assured and your mark on history is indelible.

Letter on the Retirement of the Chancellor of West Germany,
October 14, 1963

Cyrille Adoula (1921–1978) was prime minister and foreign minister of the Republic of the Congo.

The difficulties of our revolutionary experience, and the experience of every other people coming into independence since the end of World War II, pale in comparison to the problems which the Congo has faced and which press upon the prime minister and his supporters.

What makes him especially welcome is the courage and the fortitude, the persistence and the judgment with which he has met these challenges—which would have overwhelmed a lesser people, a lesser country, a lesser man, a lesser government....

We welcome you because of your own extraordinary record—rising because of your own efforts to a position of preeminence, where you have won the support of people, both within and without your country—and because of your own personal qualities.

Toast to the prime minister of the Congo, February 5, 1962

Rómulo Betancourt (1908–1981) was two-time president of Venezuela, initially through a military coup.

You represent all that we admire in a political leader. Your liberal leadership of your country, your persistent determination to make a better life for your people, your long fight for democratic leadership not only in your own country but in the entire area of the Caribbean, your companionship with other liberal progressive leaders of this hemisphere, all these have made you, for us, a symbol of what we wish for our own country and for our sister republics.

Remarks to the president of Venezuela, February 19, 1963

Habib Bourguiba (1903–2000) served for thirty years as the first president of Tunisia and was regarded as a principal voice of moderation in the Arab world.

Like President Washington, President Bourguiba is a revolutionary, and like President Washington, he also, when the revolution was won, had the sense of judgment, self-discipline and strength to attempt to bring good will and peace among his people and to the people of the former occupiers of his country and his surrounding neighbors.

As we look back in our own history, there is a glow around the names of [George] Washington, [Alexander] Hamilton, [Thomas] Jefferson and all the others who contributed to the founding of our country. We are in the presence tonight of a man who has played a comparable role in the life of his own country.

He spent many months and years in prison, and yet under great pressure and with great temptation to take the easy way, he continued to fight for the independence of his country, the peace of North Africa, for the well-being of his people.

> Toast to the president of Tunisia, May 3, 1961

Fidel Castro (1926–) came to power in Cuba as a revolutionary and nationalist in 1959 but soon became a communist who bedeviled the Kennedy administration and its successors.

Even in Cuba, Mr. Castro's emphasis, certainly at the beginning, was on a desire to improve the lot of the Cuban people.

> Remarks to governmental summer interns, June 20, 1962

I would not want to characterize Mr. Castro except to say that by his own words he has indicated his hostility to democratic liberal leaders in many of the countries of the hemisphere who are attempting to improve the life of their people, and has associated himself most intimately with the Sino-Soviet bloc, and has indicated his desire to spread the influence of that bloc throughout this hemisphere.

> Press conference, April 12, 1961

Sir Winston Churchill (1874–1965) served as a cabinet minister and prime minister of Great Britain.

I would be delighted if Congress passed a resolution, whether it's honorary citizenship or an expression of esteem [for Sir Winston Churchill]— some way or other…to remind him of our regard.

> Press conference, January 24, 1963

Whenever and wherever tyranny threatened, he has always championed liberty. Facing firmly toward the future, he has never forgotten the past.

Serving six monarchs of his native Great Britain, he has served all men's freedom and dignity.

In the dark days and darker nights when England stood alone—and most men save Englishmen despaired of England's life—he mobilized the English language and sent it into battle. The incandescent quality of his words illuminated the courage of his countrymen.

Indifferent himself to danger, he wept over the sorrows of others.

Conferring honorary citizenship on Winston Churchill,
April 9, 1963

Jacques-Yves Cousteau (1910–1997) of France, a former naval officer, was the world's best-known ocean explorer.

And the captain has given us a possibility that some day we may swim as well as the fish—or at least deeper. And he is, therefore, one of the great explorers of an entirely new dimension, and I can imagine his satisfaction in having opened up the ocean floor to man and to science.

Remarks on awarding the National Geographic Society
Gold Medal, April 19, 1961

General Charles de Gaulle (1890–1970) was the leader of the French resistance to the Nazis during World War II and served as president and prime minister of France in the postwar era.

We admire the vision of President de Gaulle, who has been able to weave from the rich heritage of France's past, the fabric of her future greatness and achievement. He has seen in the past the promise of the future, and has taken his place among those few statesmen of the West, who grasped the possibilities and meaning of history, and thus were able to shape the ultimate course for our own society.

Remarks at the opening of the Mona Lisa exhibit, National
Gallery of Art, January 8, 1963

Your personal achievements in bringing the resurgence of France as a great champion of freedom have won the esteem of all those who cherish liberty.

Message to Charles de Gaulle, April 24, 1961

In General de Gaulle, I am having a conversation with the only active figure who played a major role in the Second World War who is now involved in major policy matters affecting the security of the Western world. President [Franklin D.] Roosevelt, Prime Minister [Winston] Churchill, Marshall [Joseph] Stalin have all disappeared from the positions of responsibility. General de Gaulle remains. And he is faithful to the same concepts of the strength of France and the unity of Europe as he has been for many years.

Press conference, June 2, 1961

That bastard de Gaulle.

Phone call to Benjamin Bradlee of *Newsweek*, May 30, 1962

Eamon de Valera (1882–1975) was the U.S.-born prime minister and then president of Ireland.

De Valera is fighting politically the same relentless battle they fought in the field during the uprising of 1916, in the war of independence and later in the civil war.

He feels that everything Ireland has ever gained has been given grudgingly and at the end of a long and bitter struggle.

Always it has been too little and too late.

He is surrounded by men of the same background in his government.... Many were in the abortive uprising of 1916. All fought in the war of independence against the Black and Tans and later in the civil war of 1922. All have been in both English and Irish prisons, and many have wounds that still ache when the cold rains come in from the west.

They have not forgotten, nor have they forgiven. The only settlement they will accept is a free and independent Ireland, free to go where it will be the master of its own destiny.

Article in the *New York Journal-American*, July 29, 1945

Because of De Valera's appeal to nationalism and his mystic hold on the hearts of the people and his practical politics, he did not lose control.
Diary entry, July 25, 1945

Dag Hammarskjöld (1905–1961] of Sweden was the second secretary-general of the United Nations and died in a plane crash while on a peace-keeping mission in the Congo.

Dag Hammarskjöld's dedication to the cause of peace, his untiring labors to achieve it, his courage under attack, his willingness to accept all responsibility in trying to strengthen the United Nations and make it a more effective instrument for the aspirations of the hundreds of millions of people around the globe who desire to live out their lives—those efforts of his are well known.
Statement on Hammarskjöld's death, September 18, 1961

Hassan II (1929–1999) became king of Morocco in 1961, and Mohammad Reza Pahlavi (1919–1980) was shah of Iran from 1941 until his ouster in 1979.

He and the shah, both of them playboys at one time, are so serious now that they are kings. They must be overcompensating.
Conversation with Benjamin Bradlee of
Newsweek, April 2, 1963

Pope John XXIII (1881–1963) was born as Angelo Roncalli, ordained a Roman Catholic priest in 1904 and elevated to the papacy in 1958.

The highest work of any man is to protect and carry on the deepest spiritual heritage of the race. To Pope John was given the almost unique gift of enriching and enlarging that tradition. Armed with the humility and calm which surrounded his earliest days, he brought compassion and an understanding drawn from wide experience to the most divisive problems of a tumultuous age. He was the chosen leader of world Catholicism, but his concern for the human spirit transcended all boundaries of belief or geography.

> Statement on the pope's death, June 2, 1963

Nikita Khrushchev (1894–1971) was premier of the Soviet Union, first secretary of the country's Communist Party, and an advocate of "peaceful coexistence" with the capitalist West.

That son of a bitch Khrushchev, he won't stop until we actually take a step that might lead to nuclear war.... There's no way you can talk that fella into stopping, until you take some really credible step, which opens up that range of possibilities.

> Comment to advisor Walt Rostow, 1961

I never met a man like this. I talked about how a nuclear exchange would kill 70 million people in ten minutes, and he just looked at me as if to say, "So what?" My impression was that he just didn't give a damn if it came to that.

> Comment to Hugh Sidey of *Time* magazine, 1961

I'm sure he's not crazy.

> Comment to advisor Kenneth O'Donnell, June 1961

Writer André Malraux (1901–1976) served as France's minister of information and then as its minister of cultural affairs.

For [Andre] Malraux has revived for our own age the Renaissance ideal of the many-sided man. In his own life as a writer, a philosopher, a statesman and a soldier, he has again demonstrated that politics and art, the life of action and the life of thought, the world of events and the world of imagination, are one.

> Remarks at the opening of the Mona Lisa exhibit, National Gallery of Art, January 8, 1963

Jawaharlal Nehru (1889–1964) was prime minister of India in its early years after independence from Great Britain.

I do not know any figure in the world who is more committed to individual liberty than Mr. Nehru, and I think the people of India are committed to maintaining their national sovereignty and supporting liberty for the individual as a personal and cultural and religious tradition. We are going to disagree, but I'm sure it's possible to disagree in the framework of not charging each other with bad faith.

Press conference, November 8, 1961

Julius Nyerere (1922–1999) was the first president of Tanganyika (now Tanzania), a post he held from 1964 to 1985.

President Nyerere led the fight, led the way, led the path to independence for his own country and has recognized, as our early Founding Fathers recognized, that that was only part of the struggle and in some ways the easiest part....

This is the great test of the statesman, to build, once independence has been achieved. Your efforts to build a cohesive, open society, a free society, based on liberal principles, and also build this society and this country as part of a larger organization of East Africa, has won the respect and admiration of the government and the people of the United States.

Remarks to the president of Tanganyika, July 15, 1963

Sarvepalli Radhakrishnan (1888–1975) was a philosopher and diplomat who served as president of India from 1962 to 1967.

You are the president of the largest democracy in the world.... a country which has occupied a position of moral leadership during the difficult days which have followed the end of the Second World War....

We are glad to have you here also, Mr. President, because of your own

long and distinguished record as a teacher, as an interpreter to all the
world of the values of your civilization and its religious and cultural traditions....

The president is a noted philosopher. When I commented on the
weather this morning, he said, "We cannot always control events, but we
can always control our attitude toward events."

Remarks to the president of India, June 3, 1963

Ibn Abd al-Aziz ibn Saud (1902–1969) was king of Saudi Arabia from 1953 to
1964, when he went into exile and his brother replaced him on the throne.

And we also know that you have been a vigilant and courageous defender of your country's sovereignty and independence. You yourself
have had a distinguished military record, and come from a race which
has been outstanding in the defense of its rights.

Toast to the king of Saudi Arabia, February 13, 1962

Haile Selassie (1892–1975) was emperor of Ethiopia from 1930 until he was
deposed in 1974.

We honor not only a distinguished leader of his country and a distinguished
world figure, but we also welcome a man whose place in history is already
assured. His memorable and distinctive appearance before the League of
Nations in the mid-thirties which so stirred the conscience of the world was
supported prior to that by action, and has been supported in its high hopes,
by the consistent support which His Imperial Majesty has given to those
efforts since the end of the Second [World] War to associate free nations
together in common enterprises ... and, perhaps most celebrated of all, his
leadership in building a community of free and independent states in Africa.

Remarks of welcome at Union Station, October 1, 1963

Marshal Josip Broz Tito (1892–1980) was an anti-Nazi resistance leader who
became the communist premier and then president of Yugoslavia after
World War II.

You have had an extraordinary career in war and peace, and while there are differences in viewpoint which separate our governments, nevertheless, this administration and my two predecessors, President Eisenhower and President Truman, all believed strongly in the independence of your country and all appreciated the extraordinary efforts you are making to maintain that independence, situated as you are in an area of great importance.

Toast to the president of Yugoslavia, October 17, 1963

Manuel Prado Ugarteche (1889–1967) served twice as president of Peru, during World War II from 1939 to 1945 and again from 1956 to 1962.

I do not know of anyone in the free world, with the possible exception of General [Charles] de Gaulle, who played a leading role in the Second World War who was a most active figure in mobilizing the republics of this hemisphere in the fighting against fascism....

You were a revolutionary figure in your youth. You spent almost a decade in exile in Paris. You were a leader in the fight against fascism. You have been a leader in the fight against communism, and you are where you began: a defender of your country's stature, a defender of the cause in which we all believe.

Toast to the president of Peru, September 19, 1961

CHAPTER 18

Reflections on Courage and Leadership

"Show me a hero and I will write you a tragedy," novelist F. Scott Fitzgerald declared in 1945. But to a country that had just emerged victorious against totalitarianism in the bloodiest war of human history, such seeming cynicism held little allure. At the age of twenty-nine the following year, John Kennedy was elected to Congress as a naval war hero. Not only was he the only veteran in the race, but he had recently been awarded a Navy and Marine Corps medal for his bravery in the PT 109 affair. Although Kennedy was always modest about this event in which he saved the lives of his crew after the Japanese sank their boat, he returned repeatedly in his speeches and writings to the broader theme of courage in democratic leadership.

It is thus no accident that while recuperating from surgery in 1955, Kennedy authored—with the help of his writing and research team—*Profiles in Courage*, which highlighted courageous U.S. senators in history, and became a best-seller. In this lively book, Kennedy praised those who "traveled the hard road" by placing principle over expediency, the good of the American nation over careerism and personal gain.

Kennedy never associated physical stamina or strength, such as he showed during wartime—with leadership. But in his view, moral and political courage are vital in a democracy because leadership necessitates rising above the "herd" of convention, safe consensus, and careerism. What distinguishes excellence from mediocrity politically, Kennedy insisted, is precisely the distinguishing feature of courage. In this regard, he saw Britain's prime minister, Winston Churchill, as a personal role model—and often told people that he had read everything that Churchill wrote.

To be sure, Kennedy's critics saw his fascination with courage as tainted with needless risk taking, and even recklessness. But undoubtedly central to our thirty-fifth president's charisma and enduring mystique was his conviction that bravery and leadership not only exist despite cynical sneers but are closely linked qualities to be celebrated in the advancement of freedom.

Summoning Courage

Great crises produce great men, and great deeds of courage.
Profiles in Courage, 1956

For courage—not complacency—is our need today—leadership, not salesmanship.
Democratic nomination acceptance speech Los Angeles,
July 15, 1960

Regardless of how persistent our diplomacy may be in activities stretching all around the globe, in the final analysis it rests upon the power of the United States, and that power rests upon the will and courage of our citizens and upon you here in this field.

The United States is the guarantor of the independence of dozens of countries stretching around the world. And the reason that we are able to guarantee the freedom of those countries and to maintain that guarantee and make it good is because of you and your comrades in arms on a dozen different forts and posts, on ships at sea, planes in the air, all of you.
Remarks to the First Armored Division, Fort Stewart,
Georgia, November 26, 1962

The sea has been a friend or an enemy of us all but it has never, since our earliest beginnings, carried special hazards for the people of this country. We started as a beachhead on this continent; our forebears came by that sea to this land. The sea has been our friend and on occasion our enemy, but to life in the sea with all of its changes and hazards was added the struggle with man, and it is that struggle of nature and man which cost us the lives of 4,500 Americans whom we commemorate today.

> Remarks at the dedication of the East Coast Memorial to the
> Missing at Sea, New York, May 23, 1963

There are many kinds of courage—bravery under fire, courage to risk reputation and friendship and career for convictions which are deeply held.

Perhaps the rarest courage of all—for the skill to pursue it is given to very few men—is the courage to wage a silent battle to illuminate the nature of man and the world in which he lives.

> Remarks on the television program "Robert Frost: American Poet,"
> February 26, 1961

I do not believe that any nation in the history of the world has buried its soldiers farther from its native soil than we Americans—or buried them closer to the towns in which they grew up....

There is no way to maintain the frontiers of freedom without cost and commitment and risk.

> Remarks at Veterans Day ceremony, Arlington, Virginia,
> November 11, 1961

This southwest United States was built by men who carried rifles and plowed their fields. They plowed their fields because they were building for the future, and they carried their rifles in order that there might be a future.

> Remarks at the airport, Fort Smith, Arkansas, October 29, 1961

On the bright side of an otherwise completely black time was the way that everyone stood up to it. Previous to that I had become somewhat cynical about the American as a fighting man. I had seen too much bellyaching and laying off. But with the chips down—that all faded away. I can now believe—which I never would have before—the (World War II) stories of Bataan and Wake.

For an American, it's got to be awfully easy or awfully tough. When it's in the middle, then there's trouble.

Letter to his parents, September 12, 1943

Our own history, perhaps better than the history of any other great country, vividly demonstrates the truth of the belief that physical vigor and health are essential accompaniments to the qualities of intellect and spirit on which a nation is built. It was men who possessed vigor and strength as well as courage and vision who first settled these shores and, over more than three centuries, subdued a continent and wrested a civilization from the wilderness.

None of that hero stuff about me. The real heroes are not the men who return but those who stay out here, like plenty of them do, two of my men included.

Letter to newspaper columnist Inga Arvad, 1943

It was physical hardihood that helped Americans in two great world wars to defeat strong and tenacious foes and make this country history's mightiest defender of freedom. And today, in our own time, in the jungles of Asia and on the borders of Europe, a new group of vigorous young Americans helps maintain the peace of the world and our security as a nation.

At the same time, young Americans are attaining new standards of excellence in athletic contests. Only last month four men ran the mile in less than four minutes in a single race. Hardly a month passes that some new record for speed or strength, stamina or competitive skill, is not shattered.

"The Vigor We Need," article in Sports Illustrated, July 16, 1962

We maintain the peace by preparing for adversity.

Remarks to allied and U.S. troops, Hanau, Germany, June 25, 1963

I have been the host of more than a dozen rather extraordinary leaders of African countries who have come to the United States in the last twelve months. I would suppose that most of them have been imprisoned at one time or another in their fight for freedom. Most of them come from countries where there is almost no higher education except in a few exceptional cases.

They are faced with, in a sense, the far more pedestrian but more difficult challenge after the fight for independence has been won, which carries its own built-in enthusiasm. They are faced with the job of building a new country, lacking skilled administrators, lacking the tradition of self-government, and they represent an extraordinary group of people.

> Remarks to student volunteers in Operation Crossroads Africa, June 22, 1962

For throughout history those who live in the most danger, those who keep watch at the gate, are always prouder, more courageous, more alive, than those who live far to the rear.

> Remarks at Tegel Airport, Berlin, Germany, June 26, 1963

One million Americans serve outside our borders, and I think that the peace of this world of ours and its security have depended in a good measure upon the members of the military of the United States. And while we are all necessarily and properly respectful and impressed with the constantly more powerful weapons which are being developed, I think it is important that we realize that it is the men who must manage them, control them and have the will to direct them.

> Remarks on the Uniformed Services Pay Raise Bill, October 2, 1963

The path we have chosen for the present is full of hazards, as all paths are—but it is the one most consistent with our character and courage as a nation and our commitments around the world. The cost of freedom is always high—but Americans have always paid it. And one path we shall never choose—and that is the path of surrender or submission.

> Speech on the Cuban Missile Crisis, October 22, 1962

A nation which has forgotten the quality of courage which in the past has been brought to public life is not as likely to insist upon or reward that quality in its chosen leaders today.

Profiles in Courage, 1956

There is no official "list" of politically courageous senators, and it has not been my intention to suggest one. On the contrary, by retelling some of the most outstanding and dramatic stories of political courage in the Senate, I have attempted to indicate that this is a quality which may be found in any senator, in any political party, and in any era.

Ibid.

Acts of political courage have not, of course, been confined to the floor of the United States Senate. They have been performed with equal valor and vigor by congressmen, presidents, governors, and even private citizens with political ambitions.

Ibid.

There are thousands of Americans who lie buried all around the globe who have been fighting for the independence of other countries and, in a larger sense, for the independence of their own.

Remarks honoring Medal of Honor recipients, May 2, 1963

Democracy means much more than popular government and majority rule, more than a system of political techniques to flatter or deceive powerful blocks of voters. A democracy that has no George Norris to point to—no monument of individual conscience in a sea of popular rule—is not worthy to bear the name.

The true democracy, living and growing and inspiring, puts its faith in the people—faith that the people will not simply elect men who will represent their views ably and faithfully, but also elect men who exercise their conscientious judgment—faith that the people will not condemn those whose devotion to principle leads them to unpopular courses, but will reward courage, respect honor, and ultimately recognize right.

Profiles in Courage, 1956

The courage of life is often a less dramatic spectacle than the courage of a final moment; but it is no less a magnificent mixture of personal consequences, in spite of all obstacles and dangers and pressures—and that is the basis of all human morality.

Ibid.

Showing Leadership

The only valid test of leadership is the ability to lead, and lead vigorously.

Democratic nomination acceptance speech,
Los Angeles, July 15, 1960

To state the facts frankly is not to despair the future nor indict the past. The prudent heir takes careful inventory of his legacies, and gives a faithful accounting to those whom he owes an obligation of trust.

Profiles in Courage, 1956

Emotions move people far more strongly than the facts.

Why England Slept, 1940

The question is how we will compromise and with whom.

Profiles in Courage, 1956

Compromise need not mean cowardice. Indeed it is frequently the compromisers and conciliators who are faced with the severest tests of political courage as they oppose the extremist views of their constituents.

Ibid.

There is always inequality in life. Some men are killed in war and some men are wounded, and some men never leave the country, and some men are stationed in the Antarctic and some are stationed in San Francisco. It's very hard in military or in personal life to assure complete equality. Life is unfair.

Press conference, March 21, 1962

All of us cannot serve in our armed forces or in the government, but there is one thing each of us can do, and that is to take part in our democracy, to participate in it, and we can do that on Tuesday…which is Election Day.

> Statement urging citizens to vote, November 3, 1962

The times require leadership which will stand against the soft winds of indifference and easy popularity and personal gain. They require leadership which is disinterested, responsible and dedicated. They require the kind of leadership which you can furnish….

I do not mean by that that you should all embark on careers in the executive or legislative branch of our national government. But all are obligated to participate in, to contribute to, the national life at all levels.

In your community, in your state and in your national government, widespread opportunities are before you.

Those among you who, because of temperament or other reasons, would not aspire to public office, can certainly be of help to responsible candidates in your own home town. Remember too, that your national government does not require the services of administrators and lawyers alone. You who possess technical abilities and training can make use of your talents to contribute materially to efficient and worthwhile government.

> Address at Holyoke Trade High School, Holyoke, Massachusetts, June 1952

Unless the United States can demonstrate a sound and vigorous democratic life, a society which is not torn apart by friction and faction, an economy which is steadily growing—unless it can do all those things we cannot continue to bear the responsibilities of leadership which I think almost alone have prevented this world of ours from being overrun.

> Address at the University of North Dakota, Grand Forks, September 25, 1963

The greatest danger of all would be to do nothing.

> Speech on the Cuban Missile Crisis, October 22, 1962

I remember reading when I was in school...that at a rally in Madison Square Garden, when President [Franklin] Roosevelt was running for a second term, some garment workers unfolded a great sign that said, "We love him for the enemies he has made."

Well, I have been making some good enemies lately. I find it rather an agreeable experience.

Campaign remarks, New York, September 14, 1960

We shall need compromises in the days ahead, to be sure. But these will be, or should be, compromises of issues, not of principles. We can compromise our political positions, but not ourselves. We can resolve the clash of interests without conceding our ideals. And even the necessity for the right kind of compromise does not eliminate the need for those idealists and reformers who keep our compromises moving ahead.

Profiles in Courage, 1956

In a world of complex and continuing problems, in a world full of frustrations and irritations, America's leadership must be guided by the light of learning and reason.

Address intended for delivery at the Trade Mart, Dallas, Texas,
November 22, 1963

Motivation, as any psychiatrist will tell us, is always difficult to assess. It is particularly difficult to trace in the murky sea of politics. Those who abandoned their state and section for the national interest—men like Daniel Webster and Sam Houston, whose ambitions for higher office could not be hidden—laid themselves open to the charge that they sought only to satisfy their ambitions for the presidency. Those who broke with their party to fight for broader principles—men like John Quincy Adams and Edmund Ross—faced the accusation that they accepted office under one banner and yet deserted it in a moment of crisis for another.

Profiles in Courage, 1956

Men's ideas change slowly, and a nation's ideas change even more slowly. It takes shocks—hard shocks—to change a nation's psychology.

Why England Slept, 1940

History will not judge our endeavors, and a government cannot be selected, merely on the basis of color or creed or even party affiliation. Neither will competence and loyalty and stature, while essential to the utmost, suffice in times such as these.

Profiles in Courage, 1956

These, then, are some of the pressures which confront a man of conscience. He cannot ignore the pressure groups, his constituents, his party, the comradeship of his colleagues, the needs of his family, his own pride in office, the necessity for compromise and the importance of remaining in office.

He must judge for himself which path to choose, which step will most help or hinder the ideals to which he is committed. He realizes that once he begins to weigh each issue in terms of his chances for re-election, once he begins to compromise away his principles on one issue after another for fear that to do otherwise would halt his career and prevent future fights for principle, then he has lost the very freedom of conscience which justifies his continuance in office.

But to decide at which point and on which issue he will risk his career is a difficult and soul-searching decision.

Ibid.

When, at some future date, the high court of history sits in judgment on each of us, recording whether in our brief span of service we fulfilled our responsibilities to the state, our success or failure, in whatever office we hold, will be measured by the answers to four questions:

First, were we truly men of courage, with the courage to stand up to one's enemies, and the courage to stand up, when necessary, to one's associates, the courage to resist public pressure as well as private greed?

Second, were we truly men of judgment, with perceptive judgment of the future as well as the past, of our own mistakes as well as the mistakes of others, with enough wisdom to know what we did not know, and enough candor to admit it?

Third, were we truly men of integrity, men who never ran out on either the principles in which we believed or the people who believed in us, men whom neither financial gain nor political ambition could ever divert from the fulfillment of our sacred trust?

Finally, were we truly men of dedication, with an honor mortgaged to no single individual or group, and compromised by no private obligation or aim, but devoted solely to serving the public good and the national interest?

Ibid.

CHAPTER 19

Science, Technology, and the Future

When Soviet cosmonaut Yuri Gagarin orbited the earth in April 1961, the event sent shock waves of worry, anger, and dismay throughout American society—from the White House on down. U.S. astronaut Alan Shepard's suborbital flight a month later was a less dramatic achievement, and his colleague John Glenn would not orbit the earth until the following year. The fear that the United States was losing the "space race" had intensified since the successful Soviet launch of Sputnik, the world's first artificial satellite, in 1957. The competition born of Cold War insecurities—coupled with the links between American space and defense industries—propelled Kennedy to propose bold new initiatives in space and science. An accelerated space program would create jobs at home—particularly in the politically valuable South—and improve America's image abroad. And while often inviting the Soviet Union to cooperate with the United States on space projects, Kennedy vowed to place an American on the moon by 1970 and *"before the Russians"*— a deadline that his science advisers doubted could be achieved.

This expanded national commitment to explore space was the highest profile of Kennedy's technological interests, but he also recognized the imperative of broad improvements in scientific education, training, and resources. For example, he regarded science as a crucial tool to improve economic productivity, as well as health care, telecommunications, weaponry, and aviation. And for the country to wield that tool effectively, Kennedy advocated increased governmental involvement with research and development.

Science, Technology, and Society

All men will benefit if we can invoke the wonders of science instead of its terrors.

> Press conference, February 21, 1962

The march of technology—affecting, for example, the foods we eat, the medicines we take and the major appliances we use in our homes—has increased the difficulties of the consumer along with his opportunities; and it has outmoded many of the old laws and regulations and made new legislation necessary....

Many of the new products used every day in the home are highly complex. The housewife is called upon to be an amateur electrician, mechanic, chemist, toxicologist, dietician and mathematician—but she is rarely furnished the information she needs to perform these tasks proficiently.

> Message to Congress on protecting the consumer interest,
> March 15, 1962

There is really not much use in having science and its knowledge confined to the laboratory unless it comes out into the mainstream of American and world life.

> Address at the University of Wyoming, Laramie,
> September 25, 1963

In the last hundred years, science has thus emerged from a peripheral concern of government to an active partner. The instrumentalities devised in recent times have given this partnership continuity and force. The question in all our minds today is how science can best continue its service to the nation, to the people, to the world, in the years to come.

I would suggest that science is already moving to enlarge its influence in three general ways: in the interdisciplinary area, in the international area and in the intercultural area.

For science is the most powerful means we have for the unification of knowledge, and a main obligation of its future must be to deal with problems which cut across boundaries, whether boundaries between the sciences, boundaries between nations or boundaries between man's scientific and his human concerns.

Address at the National Academy of Sciences, October 22, 1963

Can we carry through in an age where we will witness not only new breakthroughs in weapons of destruction—but also a race for mastery of the sky and the rain, the ocean and the tides, the far side of space and the inside of men's minds?

Democratic nomination acceptance speech,
Los Angeles, July 15, 1960

Because of the ingenuity of science and man's own inability to control his relationships one with another, we happen to live in the most dangerous time in the history of the human race.

Press conference, October 11, 1961

Inevitably as the century goes on, in my judgment, machines [in the workplace will] increasingly take the place of men. Therefore, we will have more leisure, and we should take those steps in the field[s] of conservation, resource development, and recreation, which will prepare us for that period. I see the time coming at the end of the century, perhaps sooner, but not now.

Press conference, October 9, 1963

The benefits of medical research transcend the boundaries of time and geography. The discoveries of the past have been the stepping stones to present day medical research just as the discoveries of our day will serve as the pathway to great new discoveries in the future....

The expansion of educational facilities to train physicians and research scientists has number one priority....

The health of our people is our nation's most precious resource. It touches every American family and every American home.

> Address marking the opening of the Albert Einstein College of
> Medicine, Bronx, New York, October 17, 1955

It has always been a source of interest to me that in the earliest days of the founding of our country there was among some of our Founding Fathers a most happy relationship, a most happy understanding of the ties which bind science and government together.

I am sure that even some of our English friends who may be here today would probably agree that the two most exceptional men of the 18th century, both in this country and I think probably in Western Europe, would have been Benjamin Franklin and Thomas Jefferson—both leading political figures of their time, both scientists, social as well as natural.

> Remarks to the National Academy of Sciences, April 25, 1961

I am announcing today that the United States will commit itself to an important new program in civilian aviation. Civilian aviation, long both the beneficiary and the benefactor of military aviation, is of necessity equally dynamic. Neither the economics nor the politics of international air competition permits us to stand still in this area.

Today the challenging new frontier in commercial aviation and in military aviation is a frontier already crossed by the military—supersonic flight.

> Commencement address at the U.S. Air Force Academy,
> Colorado Springs, June 5, 1963

Progress in applied science and technology upon which the country relies for military strength, medical advances and the development of our civilian economy is heavily dependent upon the continuous flow of new scientific knowledge. Basic research efforts need to keep pace with our rapidly growing applied scientific activities.

Universities and technical institutions have been the principal source of this basic knowledge. About half of all basic research is carried out in academic institutions. The government has also maintained its own re-search laboratories....

In addition to supporting research, grants to universities are vitally important because of the close relationship which research bears to graduate education and to the development of an adequate supply of trained scientists and engineers.

> Letter to Congress concerning research grants to colleges and
> universities, May 23, 1962

The pace of scientific progress quickens by the year in every segment of the economy, in communications and transportation, manufacturing, medicine, agriculture and defense. There is hardly a human life or an American occupation untouched by this advance which is capable over the long run of creating a general abundance unprecedented in human history.

> Labor Day statement, September 3, 1962

Knowledge is power, and I think the events of the past years have shown that in a very dramatic way. I am particularly interested in the progress we can make in the developing countries—Latin America, Africa and Asia.

The need for trained men and women in all the disciplines of life, constantly increasing as technology and science expand our horizons, and the relatively small educated elite which we find in these countries on whom heavy burdens have been placed, I think, indicate how essen-tial it is in the sixties that the universities of the West, particularly in the highly developed countries, concentrate their attention on expanding education, indicating that education is not merely a means and an end, and not merely a technique, but also a way to the good life which is a way to a more secure afterlife.

> Remarks to convention attendees of the International Federation
> of Catholic Universities, September 4, 1963

There is indeed an explosion of knowledge and its outward limits are not yet in sight. In some fields, progress seems very fast; in others, distressingly slow. It is no tribute to modern science to jump lightly to the conclusion that all its secrets of particle physics, of molecular life, of heredity, of outer space, are now within easy reach. The truth is more massive and less magical. It is that wherever we turn, in defense, in space, in medicine, in industry, in agriculture, and most of all in basic science itself, the requirement is for better work, deeper understanding, higher education.

Address at Boston College Centennial ceremonies,
Newton, Massachusetts, April 20, 1963

Despite the striking fact that most of the scientists that the world has ever known are alive and working today, despite the fact that this nation's own scientific manpower is doubling every twelve years in a rate of growth more than three times that of our population as a whole, despite that, the vast stretches of the unknown and the unanswered and the unfinished still far outstrip our collective comprehension.

No man can fully grasp how far and how fast we have come, but condense, if you will, the 50,000 years of man's recorded history in a time span of but a half-century. Stated in these terms, we know very little about the first forty years except at the end of them advanced man had learned to use the skins of animals to cover them. Then about ten years ago, under this standard, man emerged from his caves to construct other kinds of shelter. Only five years ago man learned to write and use a cart with wheels.

Christianity began less than two years ago. The printing press came this year, and then less than two months ago, during this whole fifty-year span of human history, the steam engine provided a new source of power. [Sir Isaac] Newton provided the meaning of gravity. Last month electric lights and telephones and automobiles and airplanes became available. Only last week did we develop penicillin and television and nuclear power, and now if America's new spacecraft succeeds in reaching Venus, we will have literally reached the stars before midnight tonight.

Address at Rice University, Houston, Texas, September 12, 1962

We have made some exceptional scientific advances in the last decade, and some of them—they are not as spectacular as the man-in-space, or as the first Sputnik, but they are important. I have said that if we could ever competitively, at a cheap rate, get fresh water from salt water, that it would be in the long-range interests of humanity which would really dwarf any other scientific accomplishments....

I think that if we could increase the techniques for improving education in uneducated sections of the world—by using the latest devices of science—that would be an extraordinary accomplishment....

My feeling is that we are more durable in the long run. These dictatorships enjoy many short-range advantages, as we saw in the thirties. But in the long run, I think our system suits the qualities and aspirations of people that desire to be their own masters. Our job is to maintain our strength until our great qualities can be brought more effectively to bear. But during the meantime, it is going to require a united effort.

Press conference, April 12, 1961

Well-trained minds are among this nation's most precious assets, among the scarcest of our resources. Attainment of our many national objectives and fulfillment of existing commitments critically depend on the quantity and on the quality of manpower in all professional fields, at all levels of training.

Statement on the report of the President's Science Advisory Committee, December 13, 1962

Space Exploration

And when we make a great national effort to make sure that free men are not second in space, we move in the same direction that Thomas Jefferson moved in when he sent Lewis and Clark to the far reaches of this country during his term of office.

Address at inaugural anniversary dinner, January 20, 1962

What is fair is that we all recognize that our failures are going to be publicized and so are our successes, and there isn't anything that anyone can do about it or should.

Press conference, May 5, 1961

If we can get to the moon before the Russians, we should.

Press conference, April 21, 1961

Until we have a man on the moon, none of us will be satisfied. But I do believe a major effort is being made. But as I said before, we started far behind, and we're going to have to wait and see whether we catch up.

But I would say that I will continue to be dissatisfied until the goal is reached. And I hope everyone working on the program shares the same view.

Press conference, October 11, 1961

This nation's space program has introduced a new dimension to progress. An increasing flow of peaceful benefits, both national and international, is materializing from our efforts to probe this new frontier....

Our intensive research and development in the field of communications satellites have brought us to the point where we are now certain of the technical feasibility of transmitting messages to any part of the world by directing them to satellites for relay.

Letter to Congress on a Communications Satellite Bill,
February 7, 1962

It is increasingly clear that the impact of Colonel [John] Glenn's magnificent achievement yesterday goes far beyond our own time and our own country. The success of this flight, the new knowledge it will give us, and the new steps which can now be undertaken will affect life on this planet for many years to come.

Press conference, February 21, 1962

The United States Congress almost unanimously made a decision that the United States would not continue to be second in space. We are second in space today because we started late. It requires a large sum of money. I don't think we should look with equanimity upon the prospect that we will be second all through the sixties and possibly the seventies. We have the potential not to be.

Press conference, April 3, 1963

Now, some people are saying that we should take the money we are putting into space and put it into housing or education. We [already] sent up a very extensive educational program. My judgment is that what would happen would be that they would cut the space program, and we would not get additional funds for education.

Press conference, April 24, 1963

I hope it will be possible for the relations between the United States and the Soviet Union to develop in such a way that the peace can be protected and that it will be possible for us to use our energies along peaceful and productive and fruitful lines.

The development of space, preventing outer space from being used as a new area of war, of course, is of the greatest possible concern to the people of this country. I am hopeful that it will be possible, if relations between our two countries can be maintained, can be channeled along peaceful lines.

Press conference, February 15, 1961

We believe that when men reach beyond this planet they should leave their national differences behind them.

Press conference, February 21, 1962

I know that many of you have your eyes fixed in space and are interested and concerned about the extraordinary accomplishment of the Soviet Union in that area. I have said from the beginning that this country started late in the 1950s. We are behind and we will be behind for a period in the future, but we are making a major effort now, and this country will be heard from in space as well as in other areas in the coming months and years.

Report to the American People on the state of the national economy, August 13, 1962

Finally, if we are to win the battle that is now going on around the world between freedom and tyranny, the dramatic achievements in space which occurred in recent weeks should have made clear to us all, as did the Sputnik in 1957, the impact of this adventure on the minds of men everywhere, who are attempting to make a determination of which road they should take....

Recognizing the head start obtained by the Soviets with their large rocket engines, which gives them many months of lead-time, and recognizing the likelihood that they will exploit this lead for some time to come in still more impressive successes, we nevertheless are required to make new efforts on our own.

For while we cannot guarantee that we shall one day be first, we can guarantee that any failure to make this effort will make us last.

We take an additional risk by making it in full view of the world, but as shown by the feat of astronaut [Alan] Shepard, this very risk enhances our stature when we are successful.

But this is not merely a race. Space is open to us now, and our eagerness to share its meaning is not governed by the efforts of others. We go into space because whatever mankind must undertake, free men must fully share.

> Message to Congress on urgent national needs, May 25, 1961

I think the American people have supported the effort in space, realizing its significance, and also that it involves a great many possibilities in the future which are still almost unknown to us and just coming over the horizon.

> Press conference, June 14, 1962

The exploration of space is a broad and varied activity and the possibilities for cooperation are many.

> Message proposing joint action in the exploration of outer space with the Soviet Union, March 18, 1962

All of us remember a few dates in this century, and those of us who were very young remember Colonel [Charles] Lindbergh's flight [across the Atlantic], and Pearl Harbor, and the end of the war—and we remember the [space] flight of Alan Shepard and Major [Virgil] Grissom, and we remember the flight of Colonel [John] Glenn.

> Remarks on presenting NASA's Distinguished Service Medal, February 23, 1962

I think before the end of the sixties we will send a man to the moon, an American, and I think in so doing it is not merely that we are interested in making this particular journey but we are interested in demonstrating a dominance of this new sea, and making sure that in this new, great, adventurous period, the Americans are playing their great role, as they have in the past.

Remarks at ceremony for astronaut L. Gordon Cooper,
May 21, 1963

CHAPTER 20

A Vision for America

Was John Kennedy a visionary more than a politician? Certainly, he came from a politically skillful and well-connected family—hardly averse to the mundane realities of getting things done through deal making and compromise. From his first congressional term onward, he showed a willingness to accept the practicalities involved in maintaining elective public office. Indeed, in Kennedy's most famous book, *Profiles in Courage*, he insisted that effective compromising is the hallmark of leadership.

Yet the more we study Kennedy's life, the more relevant—and compelling—this primary question becomes. And does his vision, born of post–World War II American optimism and his own buoyant personality, remain our thirty-fifth president's most important legacy today? Historians will undoubtedly debate Kennedy's varied accomplishments, domestically and internationally, vigorously for many decades to come. But we are convinced that his most enduring impact lies precisely in the broader way that he regarded the United States in the world and expressed that viewpoint in his carefully chosen words and unique personal style.

What was the essence of Kennedy's vision? What were its specific contours? What made it so appealing, even inspirational to an entire generation? And how does it still resonate now in a time in some ways quite different from the middle decades of the twentieth century? Such questions are both tantalizing and important as we examine his loftiest perspective.

Wisdom requires the long view.
> Address at the University of California at Berkeley,
> March 23, 1962

Our goal is to influence history instead of merely observing it.
> Campaign remarks, New York, September 14, 1960

I believe the times demand invention, innovation, imagination, decision.
> Democratic nomination acceptance speech, Los Angeles,
> July 15, 1960

Whether you are citizens of America or citizens of the world, ask of us here the same high standards of strength and sacrifice which we ask of you. With a good conscience our only sure reward, with history as the final judge of our deeds, let us go forth to lead the land we love, asking His blessing and His help, but knowing that here on earth God's work must truly be our own.
> Inaugural Address, January 20, 1961

Every generation faces different problems and every generation must come up with new solutions.
> Remarks at City Hall, McKeesport, Pennsylvania, October 13, 1962

I think in these years of great hazard for our country, where we are faced with many challenges, and also I believe many opportunities, that we take our lesson and our theme from the Bible and the story of Nehemias, which tells us that when the children of Israel returned from captivity they determined to rebuild the walls of Jerusalem, in spite of the threats of the enemy. The wall was built and the peace was preserved. But it was written, "Of them that built on the wall... with one of his hands he did the work, and with the other he held the sword."

We hold the sword, and we are determined to maintain our strength and our commitments. But we also hold in our hand the trowel. We are determined to build in our own country, so that those who come after us—as they surely will—will find available to them all of the great resources that we now have.

Speech at the opening of the Ouachita National Forest Road,
Big Cedar, Oklahoma, October 29, 1961

The most powerful single force in the world today is neither communism nor capitalism, neither the H-bomb nor the guided missile—it is man's eternal desire to be free and independent.

U.S. Senate speech, July 2, 1957

The world is engaged in the most difficult and trying struggle in its long history. All of the great epics which have torn the world for the last 2,000 years pale in comparison to the great ideological gulf which separates us from those who oppose us. It is our responsibility not merely to denounce our enemies and those who make themselves our enemies but to make this system work, to demonstrate what freedom can do, what those who are committed to freedom and the future can do....

And unless in this free country of ours we are able to demonstrate that we are able to make this society work and progress, unless we can hope that from you we are going to get back all the talents which society has helped to develop in you, then, quite obviously, all the hopes of all of us that freedom will not only endure but prevail, of course, will be disappointed.

Remarks to the national convention of the Catholic Youth
Organization, New York, November 15, 1963

Much time has passed since the first colonists came to rocky shores and dark forests of an unknown continent, much time since President Washington led a young people into the experience of nationhood, much time since President Lincoln saw the American nation through the ordeal of fraternal war—and in these years our population, our plenty and our power have all grown apace....

Yet as our power has grown, so has our peril. Today we give our thanks, most of all, for the ideals of honor and faith we inherit from our forefathers—for the decency of purpose, steadfastness of resolve and strength of will, for the courage and the humility which they possessed and which we must seek every day to emulate.

Thanksgiving Day proclamation, November 5, 1963

Liberty is not easy to find. It is a search that takes us on a hard road.

Remarks at Medal of Freedom presentation, February 21, 1961

One of the great things about this country has been that our most extraordinary accomplishments have not come from the government down, or from the top down, but have come from the bottom up.

Remarks to the International Association of Machinists, May 5, 1963

"The youth of a nation," said [British Prime Minister Benjamin] Disraeli, "are the trustees of posterity." The future promise of any nation can be directly measured by the present prospects of its youth.

This nation—facing increasingly complex economic, social and international challenges—is increasingly dependent on the opportunities, capabilities and vitality of those who are soon to bear its chief responsibilities. Such attributers as energy, a readiness to question, imagination and creativity are all attributes of youth that are also essential to our national character.

Message to Congress on the nation's youth, February 14, 1963

History is what men make of it—and we would be foolish to think that we can realize our own vision of a free and diverse future without unceasing vigilance, discipline and labor.

Article in *Look* magazine, "Where We Stand," January 15, 1963

The men who first shaped the democratic legacy that you honor tonight were filled with a sense of excitement and of wonder at the importance of the events in which they were participating. It was not only, as John Adams exalted, that they were to have the unique opportunity to write a new Constitution and form a new government and begin a new nation;

it was also the deep conviction, as later expressed by Walt Whitman, that here we have planted the standard of freedom, and here we will test the capacities of men for self-government.

America was to be the great experiment, a testing ground for political liberty, a model for democratic government, and although the first task was to mold a nation on these principles here on this continent, we would also lead the fight against tyranny on all continents.

> Remarks to the Anti-Defamation League of B'nai B'rith,
> January 31, 1963

The times are too grave, the challenge too urgent, and the stakes too high—to permit the customary passions of political debate....

The problems are not all solved and the battles are not all won—and we stand today on the edge of a New Frontier—the frontier of the 1960s—a frontier of unknown opportunities and perils—a frontier of unfulfilled hopes and dreams.

> Democratic nomination acceptance speech,
> Los Angeles, July 15, 1960

We are a revolutionary country and a revolutionary people....

I must say as an American that I can think that all of us in this country can find continued inspiration and I think all of you who are citizens of countries who have newly emerged to freedom, can find some inspiration in the Farewell Address of George Washington.

Washington wrote the address in 1796, in order to eliminate himself as a candidate for a third term, but most importantly to give some guidance to our new republic. His text, his speech, is alive with the spirit of liberty. It speaks of a union of states as a political fortress against the batteries of internal and external enemies. It counsels against adopting hasty improvisations at the expense of principles which thus might undermine what cannot be directly overthrown.

There is wisdom and foresight in Washington's instructions to cherish public credit and to promote as an object of primary importance institutions for the general diffusion of knowledge.

Washington told our forefathers in this country to reject permanent, inveterate antipathies against particular nations and passionate attachments for others, and said any nation failing in this is in some degree a slave. He warned against foreign influences which seek to tamper with domestic factions, to practice the arts of seduction, to mislead public opinion.

Remarks marking African Freedom Day, April 15, 1961

For the great enemy of the truth is very often not the lie—deliberate, contrived and dishonest—but the myth—persistent, persuasive and unrealistic. Too often we hold fast to the clichés of our forebears. We subject all facts to a prefabricated set of interpretations. We enjoy the comfort of opinion without the discomfort of thought.

Mythology distracts us everywhere—in government as in business, in politics as in economics, in foreign affairs as in domestic affairs.

Commencement address at Yale University,
New Haven, Connecticut, June 11, 1962

The genius of our scientists has given us the tools to bring abundance to our land, strength to our industry and knowledge to our people. For the first time we have the capacity to strike off the remaining bonds of poverty and ignorance—to free our people for the spiritual and intellectual fulfillment which has always been the goal of our civilization.

Yet at this very moment of maximum opportunity, we confront the same forces which have imperiled America throughout its history—the alien forces which once again seek to impose the despotisms of the Old World on the people of the New.

Address to members of Congress and the diplomatic corps of
Latin America, March 13, 1961

Progress represents the combined will of the American people, and only when they are joined together for action, instead of standing still and thinking that everything that has to be done has been done. It's only when they join together in a forward movement that this country moves ahead and that we prepare the way for those who come after us.

Remarks at the groundbreaking for the San Luis Dam,
Los Banos, California, August 18, 1962

The great strength of this country is unlimited if this country makes up its mind that as a country it's going to move forward. Not the president, not the senators, not the congressmen, not the governors, not the commissioners, not the mayors but 180 million Americans can advance this country into a bright future.

> Remarks after inspecting western conservation projects,
> Fresno, California, August 18, 1962

Today, some few may try to maintain the fiction that they are of purer stock or superior breed, but their pretense is transparent. The nation got a hearty chuckle when FDR addressed the Daughters of the American Revolution as "fellow immigrants."

> Speech before a meeting of the Washington, D.C., chapter of the
> American Jewish Committee, June 4, 1957

I believe in an America where religious intolerance will someday end—where all men and all churches are treated as equal—where every man has the same right to attend or not to attend the church of his choice—where there is no Catholic vote, no anti-Catholic vote, no bloc voting of any kind—and where Catholics, Protestants and Jews, both the lay and the pastoral level, will refrain from those attitudes of disdain and division which have so often marred their works in the past, and promote instead the American ideal of brotherhood....

This is the kind of America in which I believe. And it represents the kind of presidency in which I believe—a great office that must be neither humbled by making it the instrument of any religious group nor tarnished by arbitrarily withholding its occupancy from the members of any religious group....

This is the kind of America I believe in—and this is the kind of America I fought for in the South Pacific and the kind my brother died for in Europe. No one suggested then that we might have a "divided loyalty," that we did "not believe in liberty" or that we belonged to a disloyal group that threatened "the freedom for which our forefathers died."

> Address to the Greater Houston Ministerial Association,
> Houston, Texas, September 12, 1960

The United States cannot afford to renounce responsibility for support of the very fundamentals which distinguish our concept of government from all forms of tyranny.

> Letter to Congress on three international human rights
> conventions, July 22, 1963

I think the United States today, while it moves in danger, and has, it is more secure than it was several years ago. It can be more secure even in the future.

So I do not look to the future with gloom. I do not regard the efforts of the national government, which represents the wishes of all the people, as a failure. I think the United States here and abroad is moving into its brightest period, and I hope the people of the United States make that choice and continue to make that choice as they have in the past—that they will continue to fulfill their responsibilities.

> Remarks at New England's Salute to the President dinner,
> Boston, October 19, 1963

There are many disadvantages which a free society bears with it in a Cold War struggle, but I believe over the long run that people do want to be free, that they desire to develop their own personalities and their own potentials, that democracy permits them to do so.

> Remarks at George Washington University, May 3, 1961

It is not [an] accident that the revolutionary spirit in the best sense which sprang out of Philadelphia and the United States has had the most profound reverberations down through the long corridors of time ever since that date.

Simon Bolívar, the [Latin American] liberator, wore next to his skin a picture of George Washington. And the heads of state who come year in and year out to Washington, and the thirty or forty new states which have been formed since the end of World War II, in nearly every case in their constitutions, in their declarations, have used phrases from our Constitution and our Declaration.

> Remarks at Independence Day celebration, Mexico City,
> June 30, 1962

The essence of free communication must be that our failures as well as our successes will be broadcast around the world. And therefore we take double pride in our successes.

Address to the National Association of Broadcasters, May 8, 1961

If change were easy, everybody would change. But if you did not have change, you would have revolution. I think that change is what we need in a changing world, and therefore when we embark on new policies, we drag along all the anchors of old opinions and old views. You just have to put up with it. Those who cannot stand the heat should get out of the kitchen.

Address to the American Foreign Service Association, July 2, 1962

For unless liberty flourishes in all lands, it cannot flourish in one....

For we live in an age of interdependence as well as independence—an age of internationalism as well as nationalism.

Address at the Paulskirche, Frankfurt, Germany, June 25, 1963

The New Frontier is here, whether we seek it or not. Beyond that frontier are uncharted areas of science and space, unsolved problems of peace and war, unconquered pockets of ignorance and prejudice, unanswered questions of poverty and surplus. It would be easier to shrink back from that frontier, to look to the safe mediocrity of the past, to be lulled by good intentions and high rhetoric—and those who prefer that course should not cast their votes for me, regardless of party.

Democratic nomination acceptance speech,
Los Angeles, July 15, 1960

As Frenchmen, I know that you take satisfaction that people around the world evoke your great motto of Liberty, Equality and Fraternity. What counts, of course, is not merely the words but the meaning behind them. We believe in liberty and equality and fraternity. We believe in life and liberty and the pursuit of happiness. And we believe that the rights of the individual are preeminent, not merely the slogans and the mottoes which are invoked across the globe by those who make themselves our adversary.

Toast to the president of France, Paris, May 31, 1961

The newspaper headlines and the television screens give us the short view. They so flood us with the stop-press details of daily stories that we lose sight of one of the great movements of history. Yet it is the profound tendencies of history and not the passing excitements that will shape our future.

The short view gives us the impression as a nation of being shoved and harried, everywhere on the defense. But this impression is surely an optical illusion....

And the long view shows us that the revolution of national independence is a fundamental fact of our era. This revolution will not be stopped. As new nations emerge from the oblivion of centuries, their first aspiration is to affirm their national identity. Their deepest hope is for a world where, within a framework of international cooperation, every country can solve its own problems according to its own traditions and ideals.

> Address at the University of California at Berkeley,
> March 23, 1962

We must have trained people—many trained people—their finest talents brought to the keenest edge. We must have not only scientists, mathematicians and technicians. We must have people skilled in the humanities. For this is not only the age of the missile and space vehicle and thermonuclear power. This is the age that can become [humanity's] finest hour in his search for companionship and understanding and brotherhood.

> Statement to the Association for Higher Education's *College and University Bulletin*, October 15, 1960

Youth is a time for direct action and simplification. To come from battlefields where sacrifice is the order of the day—to come from there to here—it is not surprising that they should question the worth of their sacrifice and feel somewhat betrayed.

> Article in *Chicago Herald Tribune*, May 3, 1945

Conceived in Grecian thought, strengthened by Christian morality and stamped indelibly into American political philosophy, the right of the individual against the state is the keystone of our Constitution. Each man is free. He is *free* in *thought*. He is *free* in *expression*. He is *free* in *worship*.

To us, who have been reared in the American tradition, these rights have become part of our very being. They have become so much a part of our being that most of us are prone to feel that they are rights universally recognized and universally exercised.

But the sad fact is that this is not true. They were dearly won for us only a few short centuries ago and they were dearly preserved for us in the days just past. And there are large sections of the world today where these rights are denied as a matter of philosophy and as a matter of government.

We cannot assume that the struggle is ended. It is never-ending.

Independence Day oration, Boston, July 4, 1946

The fact of the matter is, as a general rule, every time we bet on the future of this country we win.

Remarks at the dedication of the Whiskeytown Dam and
Reservoir, Shasta County, California, September 28, 1963

America today is a product of its immigrants—and a product that is the envy of the world. We recognize that the new amalgamated man, a strictly made-in-America product, is the stronger and fresher because he has borrowed the best strains of many lands.

Speech before a meeting of the Washington, D.C., chapter of the
American Jewish Committee, June 4, 1957

When history writes its verdict, let it say that we pursued peace with all of our courage, that we did everything that we could do in our hands to make sure that the blessing was brought to our children and all those who think as we do. We are, in this country, the youngest of people—but we are the oldest of republics. Now is our chance, in this country, to extend the hand of friendship to the oldest of people and the youngest of republics.

Speech before a meeting of the Zionist Organization of America,
New York, August 1960

Today our concern must be with the future. For the world is changing. The old era is ending. The old ways will not do.

Democratic nomination acceptance speech, Los Angeles,
July 15, 1960

We cannot be satisfied with things as they are. We cannot be satisfied to drift, to rest on our oars, to glide over a sea whose depths are shaken by subterranean upheavals.

> Campaign remarks, Syracuse, New York, September 19, 1960

The new pioneer must be [one] who knows where he is going and how he is going about it. Trial and error is a perilous process when a single misstep can bring the holocaust that can end our efforts.

> Statement to the Association for Higher Education's *College and University Bulletin*, October 15, 1960

We are a great and strong country—perhaps the greatest and strongest in the history of the world. But greatness and strength are not our natural rights. They are not gifts which are automatically ours forever. It took toil and courage and determination to build this country—and it will take those same qualities if we are to maintain it. For, although a country may stand still, history never stands still.

> Campaign remarks, Raleigh, North Carolina, September 17, 1960

I believe…in the United States of America, in the promise that it contains and has contained throughout our history of producing a society so abundant and creative and so free and responsible that it cannot only fulfill the aspirations of its citizens, but serve equally well as a beacon for all mankind.

> Acceptance speech to the Liberal Party, New York, September 14, 1960

Today, I believe…the proudest boast is to say, "I am a citizen of the United States." And it is not enough to merely say it; we must live it.

> Remarks at City Hall Plaza, New Orleans, May 4, 1962

References

* * * * *

Bradlee, Benjamin C. *Conversations with Kennedy.* New York: Norton, 1975.

Carruth, Gorton and Eugene Ehrlich. *The Giant Book of American Quotations.* New York: Portland House, 1988.

Chase, Harold W., and Allen H. Lerman, eds. *Kennedy and the Press: The News Conferences.* New York: Thomas Y. Crowell, 1965.

Claflin, Edward B. *JFK Wants to Know: Memos from the President's Office 1961–1963.* New York: Morrow, 1991.

Dallek, Robert. *An Unfinished Life: John F. Kennedy, 1917–1963.* Boston: Little, Brown, 2003.

Damore, Leo. *Cape Cod Years.* Englewood Cliffs, NJ: Prentice-Hall, 1967.

Donald, Aïda DiPace. *John F. Kennedy and the New Frontier.* New York: Hill and Wang, 1966.

Gardner, Gerald, ed. *The Shining Moments: The Words and Moods of John F. Kennedy.* Montreal, Canada: Pocket Books, 1964.

Hamilton, Nigel. *JFK: Reckless Youth.* New York: Random House, 1992.

Israel, Fred I, ed. *The State of the Union Messages of the Presidents 1790–1966,* vol. 3, 1905–1966. New York: Chelsea House Publishers, 1967.

Jones, Charles O. *Preparing to Be President: The Memos of Richard E. Neustadt.* Washington, DC: AEI Press, 2000

Kemper, Deane Alwyn. *John F. Kennedy before the Greater Houston Ministerial Association, September 12, 1960: The Religious Issue.* Ph.D. diss. Michigan State Univ., 1968

Kennedy, John F. *Why England Slept.* New York: Wilfred Funk, 1940.

——"New England and the South." *Atlantic Monthly,* January 1954.

——*Profiles in Courage.* New York: Harper & Brothers, 1956.

——*The Strategy of Peace.* Edited by Allan Nevins. New York: Harper & Brothers, 1960.

——*President Kennedy's Proposals.* Washington, DC: Congressional Quarterly Service, May 1961.

——*Public Papers of the Presidents of the United States, 1961.* U.S. Government Printing Office, 1962.

——*Creative America.* New York: Ridge Press, 1962

——*To Turn the Tide.* Edited by John W. Gardner. New York: Harper & Brothers, 1962.

——*Public Papers of the Presidents of the United States, 1962.* U.S. Government Printing Office, 1963.

——*Public Papers of the Presidents of the United States, 1963.* U.S. Government Printing Office, 1964.

——*America the Beautiful in the Words of John F. Kennedy.* Elm Grove, WI: Country Beautiful Foundation, 1964.

——*A Nation of Immigrants.* New York: Harper & Row, 1964.

——*The Kennedy Wit.* Edited by Bill Adler. New York: Citadel Press, 1964.

——*John F. Kennedy on Israel, Zionism, and Jewish Issues.* New York: Herzl Press, 1965.

——*More Kennedy Wit.* Edited by Bill Adler. New York: Bantam, 1965.

——*Prelude to Leadership: The European Diary of John F. Kennedy, Summer 1945.* Washington, DC: Regnery Publishing, 1995.

Milton, Joyce. *John F. Kennedy.* London: DK Publishing, 2003.

O'Donnell, Kenneth P., and Dave F. Powers. *Johnny, We Hardly Knew Ye.* Boston: Little, Brown, 1970.

O'Hara, William T. *John F. Kennedy on Education.* New York: Teachers College Press, 1966.

Parmet, Herbert S. *Jack: The Struggles of John F. Kennedy.* New York: Dial Press, 1980.

——*JFK: The Presidency of John F. Kennedy.* New York: Dial Press. 1983.

Podell, Janet, and Steven Anzovin, eds. *Speeches of the American Presidents*. New York: H. W. Wilson, 1988.

Reeves, Richard. *President Kennedy: Profile of Power*. New York: Simon & Schuster, 1993.

Reeves, Thomas C. *A Question of Character: A Life of John F. Kennedy*. New York: Crown Forum, 1997.

Ryan, Halford, ed. *The Inaugural Addresses of Twentieth-Century American Presidents*. Westport, CT: Praeger, 1993.

Sanghvi, Ramesh. *John F. Kennedy: A Political Biography*. Bombay, India: Perennial Press, 1961.

Schneider, Nicholas A., comp. *Religious Views of President John F. Kennedy in His Own Words*. St. Louis, MO: Herder Books, 1965.

Wicker, Tom. *JFK and LBJ: The Influence of Personality upon Politics*. New York: Morrow, 1968.

Index

★ ★ ★ ★ ★

About the Editors

* * * * *

ERIC FREEDMAN, J.D., is a Pulitzer Prize–winning reporter and an assistant professor of journalism at Michigan State University. He is a former congressional aide and Fulbright scholar in Uzbekistan. He has written books on higher education, history, travel, and natural resources, and conducts research about public affairs reporting in the United States and about press restraints and journalism in Central Asia.

EDWARD HOFFMAN, PH.D., is an adjunct psychology professor at Yeshiva University and a licensed New York State psychologist. He is the author editor of more than a dozen books, including award-winning biographies of psychologists Abraham Maslow and Alfred Adler. He also edited several anthologies, including *The Book of Fathers' Wisdom, The Book of Graduation Wisdom, Future Visions: The Unpublished Papers of Abraham Maslow,* and *The Wisdom of Carl Jung.* Dr. Hoffman lectures widely on humanistic psychology throughout the United States and abroad, and his books have been translated into many languages.